BUTTER BOARDS

BUTTER BOARDS

13-Digit ISBN: 978-1-64643-422-0
10-Digit ISBN: 1-64643-422-6

This book may be ordered by mail from the publisher. Please include $5.99 for postage and handling.

Please support your local bookseller first!

Books published by Cider Mill Press Book Publishers are available at special discounts for bulk purchases in the United States by corporations, institutions, and other organizations. For more information, please contact the publisher.

Cider Mill Press Book Publishers
"Where good books are ready for press"
501 Nelson Place
Nashville, Tennessee 37214

cidermillpress.com

Typography: IvyMode, Sofia Pro

Image Credits: Pages 8, 41, 111 used under official license from Shutterstock.com. Page 183 used under official license from Unsplash.com. All other photos courtesy of Alejandra Diaz-Imlah.

Printed in Malaysia

23 24 25 26 27 OFF 5 4 3 2 1
First Edition

BUTTER BOARDS

50+ INVENTIVE SPREADS FOR ENTERTAINING

ALEJANDRA DIAZ-IMLAH and JAMISON DIAZ-IMLAH

CIDER MILL PRESS

BOOK PUBLISHERS

CONTENTS

INTRODUCTION

Whether it's a cheese board, a charcuterie board, or a dessert board, a board freighted with delicious items is always a hit. While those are all tried-and-true boards and platters, a new and increasingly popular trend is the butter board. Simply put, a butter board consists of softened butter that is spread on a board and can be paired with different ingredients to provide a fun, unexpected, and creative way to serve a large group. On top of everything else, a butter board is incredibly easy to prepare.

While butter boards found a new level of popularity in 2022, mainly as a TikTok trend kicked off by content creator Justine Doiron, chef Joshua McFadden is the real innovator in the space, and has been making butter boards for about a decade now.

When you first encounter a butter board, it can look a bit over-the-top. But the moment you swipe some of that butter on a piece of bread or a cracker, you get a comforting, familiar feeling. After all, we all know and love bread and butter.

This book will teach you how to make the most of various butters, showing you different methods and approaches you can use to create memorable butter boards. What's great is that you can scale them up or down, depending on group size. You can also emphasize a particular season, or articulate a theme and create a brunch board, or even a birthday board. The opportunities for the imaginative host are endless.

SELECTING INGREDIENTS

The butters featured in this book play on different seasons, themes, and traditional dishes, and are paired with complementary recipes to show you how easy and fun it is to create cohesive butter boards. As you'll see, you can compose sweet boards with toppings such as chocolate, fruits, jams, and citrus, and savory boards with vegetables, peppers, herbs, and seasonings. There are also plenty of options for serving with the various butters, including focaccia, pita chips, naan, fresh veggies, and many more. That said, there are some ingredients that are helpful to always have on hand, including a variety of salts, fresh herbs, bread, crackers, Garlic Confit (see page 18), and, of course, room-temperature butter.

When choosing the butter for your board, you want to ensure that it's unsalted and softened to room temperature. This softened butter will give you the right foundation to build a butter board upon. Having the right consistency of the butter is key. The easiest way to soften it is by leaving it out at room temperature for at least 30 minutes. You could also leave the butter out overnight. You just want to make sure that you never melt the butter, so it's recommended to keep it out of the microwave, which tends to melt some portion of the butter before all of it is fully softened.

While we use a couple of different butters in the boards here, we tend to start with unsalted butter as the base because of its consistency and versatility when pairing with other ingredients—remember, you can always add salt.

If you're looking to mix things up, you could also use other types of butter as your base, depending on your preferences. The following are some good options:

CULTURED BUTTER

A creamier butter that has a tangier, more pronounced butter flavor because of the addition of live bacterial cultures and the absence of the sweet cream used in most butters on the American market. Because of its more acidic, yogurt-like flavor, cultured butter will work best on savory boards.

IRISH BUTTER

A butter with a higher fat and lower water content compared to American butter, it tends to be richer and creamier in texture and noticeably yellower.

EUROPEAN BUTTER

Similar to Irish butter in terms of richness, this butter is most commonly unsalted and cultured.

PLANT-BASED BUTTER

Butter produced from oils in plants can be used to make vegan-friendly butter boards.

HOW TO CREATE THE PERFECT BUTTER BOARD

The obvious choice for serving is a wooden board, but there is actually an array of surfaces you could use, from trays and ceramic plates to stone boards. This is also where the fun begins. You set the mood by selecting your board and props to create the feeling you want your guests to have. Don't be afraid to mix and match materials and textures and use props such as knives, linens, small bowls, and/or plates. As with a charcuterie board, a successful butter board is all about playing into a theme, so don't hesitate to go all out—you could even search color mood boards to ensure your butter board feels cohesive.

You can go with a lighter or darker wooden board, but it all depends on your ingredients. Are your ingredients more on the darker side? Then perhaps a lighter board will make them pop. Do you have a wooden board with an orange hue? Then use that board for ingredients that have more neutral undertones. Overall, wooden boards are a great option if you want a homey, rustic vibe.

Marble and stone boards tend to go best with themes that are light and vibrant, as they really make bold colors pop. Think of a spring-themed board or citrus-based board where the colors of the complementary ingredients will stand out, but the overall feel remains fresh. One thing to keep in mind about a stone board—marble in particular—is how porous it is. To be safe, make sure not to have butters infused with colorful ingredients, such as a beet-based butter, on it for long periods of time.

Using ceramics provides so many options, since you could use small or large ceramic plates, trays, or platters. These tend to have texture and pair nicely with other materials. A tip here is to go with a neutral white, gray, or beige so as not to take attention away from the butter and other items.

This may seem a bit out there, but large square or rectangular floor tiles actually make for really nice boards. They often have so much texture to them, and offer a number of different materials. You can grab sample ones from your nearest hardware store, and as long as you give them a good wash and ensure that no particles will get on your food, you're good to go.

ASSEMBLING A BUTTER BOARD

Aside from enjoying your creation, the best part of a butter board is putting it all together. The first step is to choose your theme, either going with one from this book or coming up with one on your own. From there, you want to think about the type of butter you want to use and what flavors it will be infused with. After that, pick your complementary items. Will the butter be served with homemade bread? Fresh vegetables or fruit? Or how about something on the sweeter side, like banana bread?

When your theme and all of your components are ready, select your serving surface and start putting it all together. For a lot of the recipes, it is recommended that you whip the butter in a stand mixer or food processor briefly before spreading. This will not only ensure that the ingredients are evenly

mixed into the butter, it also incorporates air into the butter, making it easier to spread. If you don't have a stand mixer, you can easily mix the butter by hand.

After whipping the butter, it's best to start with spreading the butter with a small knife or spatula, and then adding any toppings and/or complementary items. You can also use cake decorating tools or patterned rubber bench scrapers to add texture into the butter when spreading.

While it's great to use a variety of ingredients and toppings when constructing a butter board, you don't want to overload the board. That's also what makes butter boards stand out from charcuterie or cheese boards. We have one main focus here, and that's the butter.

Lastly, set any additional tools, such as your serving knives and spoons, on the table. You can even create some ambiance by placing linens underneath the board, or placing some candles and flowers on the table, to make the board feel like a special occasion.

SERVING AND STORING

One of the many things that's great about butter boards is that you can make the butter beforehand. If you have an event coming up, you can make your butter, store it in an airtight container in the freezer, and then pull it out and let it soften to room temperature while you make the complementary items. Freezing the butter is also a good tip if you're putting a board together at a friend's or family member's home. The same goes for any leftover butter. Freezing butter should be your go-to time-saver.

SAVORY

Butter, with its rich, creamy flavor, was made
to match with savory preparations. In this chapter
you'll find a collection of simple boards that
make the most of this natural affinity.

ROASTED GARLIC BUTTER WITH GARLIC CONFIT & CRACKERS

This board is an elevated take on garlic bread, and one that is sure to wow your friends and family. By using Garlic Confit in place of raw, chopped garlic, you get all of the deep flavor and none of the harsh bite, and become acquainted with an ingredient that you will find no shortage of uses for.

4 oz. unsalted butter, softened

2 tablespoons Garlic Confit (see page 18), plus more, lightly crushed, for garnish

¼ teaspoon kosher salt

Fresh thyme, for garnish

Crackers or bread, for serving

1   Place the butter in the work bowl of a stand mixer fitted with the paddle attachment, then add the Garlic Confit and salt.

2   Mix on medium-low for about 1 minute, or until the Garlic Confit has broken down and become blended into the butter.

3   Use a rubber spatula to scrape down the side and bottom of the mixing bowl. Mix again on medium for another 15 to 30 seconds to ensure that all of the butter gets evenly incorporated.

4   After all of the butter is evenly mixed with the Garlic Confit, spread it on a board in your desired manner. Garnish with thyme and additional Garlic Confit and serve with crackers or bread.

Pro tip: the oil that the garlic sits in also makes for a wonderful condiment.

GARLIC CONFIT

Extra-virgin olive oil, as needed

Cloves from 5 heads of garlic

Salt, to taste

Pinch of red pepper flakes

Zest of ½ lemon

12 sprigs of fresh thyme

1 Warm a heavy-bottomed pot over medium-high heat and add enough olive oil to coat the bottom. Add the garlic.

2 Cook the garlic on medium heat for about 10 minutes, stirring occasionally and checking the heat to ensure the garlic is cooking evenly, until the garlic is a beautiful golden brown on all sides.

3 Add salt and the red pepper flakes. Stir to distribute.

4 Add olive oil until it fully covers the garlic. Add the lemon zest and thyme and turn the heat down to the lowest setting.

5 Continue to cook the garlic on very low heat for 20 to 30 minutes, or until the garlic is tender enough that you can easily crush it with a fork.

6 Store the garlic, covered in the oil, in the refrigerator until ready to serve. The garlic confit will keep in the refrigerator for up to 2 months.

BACON BUTTER WITH BACON & MAPLE BISCUITS

Thanks to its velvety texture and rich flavor, bacon fat is a natural to be turned into a buttery spread. In addition, these biscuits are a perfect complement, with the right amount of sweetness to cut through all of the bacon.

4 oz. bacon fat, at room temperature

Maple syrup, for garnish

Bacon & Maple Biscuits (see page 22), for serving

1   Place the bacon fat in the work bowl of a stand mixer fitted with the paddle attachment and mix on medium-low for about 1 minute, or until the fat seems light and airy and is spreadable.

2   Spread the butter on a board in the desired manner, garnish with a drizzle of maple syrup, and serve with the Bacon & Maple Biscuits.

BLT BOARD

If you want, you can also use the Bacon Butter on a board that is an homage to the classic BLT sandwich. To make this lunch-friendly board, spread the Bacon Butter on a board and serve with sliced tomatoes, fresh lettuce leaves, crispy bacon, and toasted bread. To make this a little bit lighter, just use the lettuce leaves to make wraps.

BACON & MAPLE BISCUITS

1   Preheat the oven to 425°F.

2   Sift the flour, baking powder, baking soda, and fine sea salt into a food processor and pulse a few times to mix the ingredients together.

3   Add the butter and bacon fat and pulse a few times until the butter breaks into pieces the size of small beans. Do not overwork the fats.

4   Transfer the mixture to a large bowl, making a well in the center as though you were making pasta dough.

5   Add the syrup, then the buttermilk, to the well and gently mix to bring everything together. The dough will still be a little wet when fully incorporated. Do not overmix, or your biscuits will be dense and tough.

6   Dust the counter with flour and transfer the dough onto it.

7   Dust the top of the dough with more flour, and, using a rolling pin, gently roll the dough so that it is about ¼ inch thick. Fold half of the dough back over itself so that it is about ½ inch thick, and gently roll the dough, pressing the two halves together. Repeat the process one more time, but this time, work the dough gently. The dough should be about ¾ to 1 inch thick.

8   Cut the biscuits into 2½ inch rounds, and place them on a baking sheet that has been buttered or lined with parchment paper. You can reroll the scraps and cut them into biscuits, but be careful not to overwork them.

9   Brush the tops of the biscuits with the egg, place them in the oven, and bake for 16 to 20 minutes, rotating the baking sheet halfway through. The biscuits are finished when they are a deep golden brown on top and no longer doughy in the middle.

10 Remove the biscuits from the oven, brush the tops with melted butter, sprinkle coarse sea salt over them, drizzle some honey over the top, and serve.

2 cups all-purpose flour,
plus more as needed

1 tablespoon baking powder

½ teaspoon baking soda

1½ teaspoons fine sea salt

6 tablespoons unsalted
butter, chilled and diced,
plus more, melted,
for topping

2 tablespoons bacon fat,
chilled

2 tablespoons maple syrup

1 cup buttermilk

1 egg, beaten

Coarse sea salt, for garnish

Honey, for topping

ORANGE & CLOVE BUTTER WITH ROASTED BEETS

A beautiful board that packs a surprising amount of flavor, and one that will provide a bit of brightness when the winter starts to wear on you. This orange-and-clove butter will serve you well throughout the holiday season, and the subtle sweetness of the Roasted Beets makes them a great option when you want a tasty snack but don't want to derail your diet.

4 oz. unsalted butter, softened

¼ teaspoon kosher salt

¼ teaspoon ground cloves

Zest of 1 orange

½ teaspoon fresh thyme, plus more for garnish

Pomegranate seeds, for garnish

Roasted Beets (see page 26), for serving

1 Place the butter in the work bowl of a stand mixer fitted with the paddle attachment and add the salt, cloves, orange zest, and thyme.

2 Mix on medium-low for about 1 minute, or until all of the ingredients have evenly blended into the butter.

3 Use a rubber spatula to scrape down the side and bottom of the mixing bowl. Mix again at medium speed for another 15 to 30 seconds to ensure that all of the butter gets evenly incorporated.

4 Spread the butter on a board in the desired manner, garnish with pomegranate seeds and additional thyme, and serve with the Roasted Beets.

ROASTED BEETS

4 small beets

Extra-virgin olive oil, as needed

Salt, to taste

1 Preheat the oven to 350°F.

2 Toss the beets in olive oil, add them to a baking dish, and wrap the pan with aluminum foil.

3 Place the dish in the oven and roast the beets for about 1½ hours, or until you can easily pierce the beets with a fork.

4 Remove the beets from the oven and immediately transfer them to a heatproof bowl. Cover the bowl with plastic and let the beets steam until they have cooled to room temperature.

5 Peel the beets and cut them to your desired size. Toss them with olive oil and salt before serving.

BBQ PORK BUTTER WITH CRACKERS

This is somewhat of a loose take on a butter board, but most people who get a taste of it love it! The pork butter is essentially rendered pork fat, spiked with BBQ-friendly spices. If you're one of those people who is a fiend for pork—or you know one of your guests is—swap the crackers out and serve pork rinds.

1 tablespoon paprika

1½ teaspoons granulated garlic

1½ teaspoons granulated onion

1½ teaspoons chili powder

1½ teaspoons coriander

1½ teaspoons dried thyme

½ teaspoon ground mustard

1½ tablespoons brown sugar

½ teaspoon kosher salt, plus more to taste

½ teaspoon cayenne pepper

½ teaspoon black pepper

4 oz. rendered pork fat, at room temperature

Crackers, for serving

1 Mix all of the ingredients, except for the pork fat and crackers, together until fully incorporated. Set ½ teaspoon of the mixture aside to use in the butter and store the rest of the spice mixture in an airtight container.

2 Add the rendered pork fat to a pot and slowly heat until it becomes a liquid.

3 Add the spice mixture and whisk it into the fat. Season with salt to taste.

4 Allow the seasoned pork fat to cool until it is no longer clear and has a texture similar to butter.

5 Spread the pork butter on a board in the desired manner and serve with crackers.

ROASTED GARLIC BUTTER WITH GARLIC & LEMON ASPARAGUS

In many places, the first things to pop up during the spring are asparagus and young garlic. This board celebrates that glorious moment when you realize that winter has completely passed.

Roasted Garlic Butter
(see page 17)

Garlic & Lemon Asparagus
(see page 32), for serving

1 Spread the butter on a board in the desired manner and serve with the Garlic & Lemon Asparagus.

GARLIC & LEMON ASPARAGUS

1 cup salt

1 lb. asparagus, trimmed

2 tablespoons
Garlic Confit (see page 18)

2 tablespoons
Garlic Confit oil

Zest of 1 lemon

Juice of ½ lemon

1 Preheat the oven to 400°F. Fill a large pot with water and bring it to a boil.

2 When the water has reached a rapid boil, add the salt to the water.

3 Allow the water to come back to a boil, then carefully add the asparagus into the water and cook for about 1½ minutes or until it becomes a bright green. It is better to undercook the asparagus than overcook it.

4 Remove the asparagus, shake off the excess water, and transfer it to a baking sheet. Add the Garlic Confit and Garlic Confit oil and toss to combine. Place the asparagus in the oven and roast it for 5 to 6 minutes, or until it just starts to color.

5 Remove the asparagus from the oven and transfer it to a serving dish. Add the lemon zest and lemon juice, toss to combine, and serve.

AUTUMN BUTTER WITH CUMIN-SCENTED BRUSSELS SPROUTS & CINNAMON-DUSTED SWEET POTATOES

This seasonally inspired butter board is a great lead-in to any of the comforting dinners that are popular once fall is in full swing.

4 oz. unsalted butter, softened

¼ teaspoon kosher salt

1 teaspoon fresh thyme

1 teaspoon chopped fresh rosemary

1 teaspoon chopped fresh sage

Cumin-Scented Brussels Sprouts (see page 36), for serving

Cinnamon-Dusted Sweet Potatoes (see page 37), for serving

1 Place the butter in the work bowl of a stand mixer fitted with the paddle attachment and add the salt, thyme, rosemary, and sage.

2 Mix on medium-low for about 1 minute, or until the butter is soft and spreadable.

3 Use a rubber spatula to scrape down the side and bottom of the mixing bowl. Mix again at medium speed for another 15 to 30 seconds to ensure that all of the butter gets evenly incorporated.

4 Spread the butter on a board in the desired manner and serve with the Cumin-Scented Brussels Sprouts and Cinnamon-Dusted Sweet Potatoes.

CUMIN-SCENTED BRUSSELS SPROUTS

1 lb. fresh Brussels sprouts, trimmed and halved

1 tablespoon extra-virgin olive oil

Salt, to taste

½ teaspoon cumin

1   Preheat the oven to 375°F.

2   Toss the Brussels sprouts with the olive oil, salt, and cumin and place them on a baking sheet.

3   Place the Brussels sprouts in the oven and roast them for about 30 to 40 minutes, or until they are roasted and cooked through.

4   Remove the Brussels sprouts from the oven and let them cool slightly before serving.

CINNAMON-DUSTED SWEET POTATOES

Extra-virgin olive oil, as needed

2 large sweet potatoes, rinsed well and scrubbed

Salt, to taste

Cinnamon, to taste

1 Preheat the oven to 375°F and coat a baking sheet with olive oil.

2 Cut each sweet potato in half lengthwise and place them, skin side up, on the baking sheet. Place the sweet potatoes in the oven and bake for 30 minutes.

3 Remove the baking sheet from the oven and flip each sweet potato so that the skin side is down and you can see the flesh of the sweet potato. Season with salt, and then sprinkle a few pinches of cinnamon over them. Drizzle olive oil over the sweet potatoes, place them back in the oven, and continue roasting for another 10 minutes, until they are fully cooked.

4 Remove the sweet potatoes from the oven and let them cool briefly before serving.

AUTUMN BUTTER WITH ROASTED ROOT VEGETABLES

This board is best for those bitterly cold nights that arrive toward the tail end of fall, when you can feel Father Winter's fast approach.

Autumn Butter (see page 35)

Lemon slices, for garnish

Roasted Root Vegetables (see page 40), chopped, for serving

1   Spread the butter on a board in the desired manner, garnish with slices of lemon, and serve with the Roasted Root Vegetables.

ROASTED ROOT VEGETABLES

1 large parsnip, peeled and sliced

2 carrots, peeled and sliced

1 celery root, peeled and sliced

1 tablespoon extra-virgin olive oil

Salt and pepper, to taste

2 sprigs of fresh rosemary, plus 1 tablespoon, chopped

2 sprigs of fresh sage, plus 1 tablespoon, chopped

2 tablespoons unsalted butter, diced

1 Preheat the oven to 400°F.

2 Place the vegetables in a bowl and toss them with the olive oil, salt, and sprigs of rosemary and sage. Place them on a baking sheet in an even layer.

3 Place the vegetables in the oven and roast them for 30 minutes, or until the vegetables are a deep golden brown and are about 90 percent of the way cooked, having just a little bit of crunch left in the center.

4 Remove the tray from the oven and evenly distribute the small pieces of butter over the vegetables.

5 Place the vegetables back in the oven and continue cooking for 5 minutes.

6 Remove the vegetables from the oven and add the chopped rosemary and sage, and stir to distribute the herbs evenly. Return the vegetables to the oven and continue cooking for 5 minutes.

7 Remove the roasted vegetables from the oven, season them with salt and pepper, and serve hot.

MEDITERRANEAN BUTTER WITH NAAN

Spiking a butter with the flavors familiar to Mediterranean cuisine calls out for olives, fresh herbs, and flatbreads. While pita is certainly an option for the latter component, we feel the buttery flavor of homemade Naan is a better fit for this board.

4 oz. unsalted butter, softened

1 tablespoon Garlic Confit (see page 18)

Zest of 1 lemon

1 teaspoon cumin

½ teaspoon paprika

⅛ teaspoon red pepper flakes

¼ teaspoon kosher salt

Fresh parsley, chopped, for garnish

Fresh basil, chopped, for garnish

8 Kalamata olives, pitted and quartered, for garnish

1 tablespoon Garlic Confit oil, for garnish

Naan (see page 44), for serving

1 Place the butter in the work bowl of a stand mixer fitted with the paddle attachment and add the Garlic Confit, lemon zest, cumin, paprika, red pepper flakes, and salt.

2 Mix on medium-low for about 1 minute, or until the confit has broken apart and become blended into the butter.

3 Use a rubber spatula to scrape down the side and bottom of the mixing bowl. Mix on medium for another 15 to 30 seconds to ensure that all of the butter gets evenly incorporated.

4 Spread the butter on a board in your desired manner. Garnish with parsley, basil, the olives, and the Garlic Confit oil and serve with the Naan.

NAAN

1 Using a small pot, add the milk and honey and gently warm to 90°F, making sure to not overheat.

2 Add the yeast to the milk and honey and whisk to dissolve. Allow the yeast to proof for 5 to 10 minutes, or until it starts to foam.

3 Once the yeast starts to foam, add the milk mixture to the work bowl of a stand mixer fitted with the dough hook, followed by the olive oil, egg, fine sea salt, and flours. Mix on low for about 3 minutes, or until a dough forms and the ball of dough no longer sticks to the side of the bowl.

4 Scrape the dough down from the dough hook, and then continue to mix on low for another minute to develop some texture in the dough.

5 Transfer the dough to a bowl that has been lightly coated with olive oil. Wrap the dough with plastic and allow it to rise at room temperature for about 1 hour, or until it doubles in size.

6 Transfer the dough to a counter and divide it into 9 equal portions of about 3 oz. each. Roll each portion into a ball and gently coat it with olive oil.

7 Loosely cover the balls of dough with plastic wrap and allow them to rise again for about 30 minutes.

8 Using either a rolling pin or the palms of your hands, flatten each ball of dough down and stretch it out, as though you were making mini pizzas. While you are flattening the balls of dough, heat a cast-iron skillet over medium-high heat.

9 Once the pan is hot, brush the flattened dough with olive oil and gently transfer it to the pan. Cook the dough on one side for about 2 to 3 minutes, or until you see nice charred spots in the dough, but before it burns. Flip the dough and continue cooking for about 1 minute, or until the dough puffs up slightly.

10 Transfer the Naan to a cutting board, brush with olive oil, and garnish with flaky sea salt. Repeat until all of the naan have been cooked and serve warm.

1 cup plus 2 tablespoons
whole milk

2 teaspoons honey

2 teaspoons active dry yeast

2 tablespoons extra-virgin
olive oil, plus more
as needed

1 egg

1 teaspoon fine sea salt

2½ cups all-purpose flour

1 cup bread flour

Flaky sea salt, for garnish

YIELD: 6 SERVINGS

CHRISTMAS BUTTER WITH RADISHES & CRANBERRIES

For this butter board, we use a different technique in order to get the butter to retain the exact shape we want. First, we whip and freeze the butter, and then we use Christmas-themed cookie cutters to cut it into festive shapes. The result is a unique butter board that is sure to get everyone in the holiday spirit.

4 oz. unsalted butter, softened

¼ teaspoon kosher salt

Fresh thyme, for garnish

Fresh sage, chopped, for garnish

Fresh rosemary, chopped, for garnish

Pomegranate seeds, for garnish

Watermelon radishes, sliced, for serving

Orange slices, for serving

Cranberry Relish (see page 162), for serving

1 Place the butter in the work bowl of a stand mixer fitted with the paddle attachment and add the salt.

2 Mix on medium-low for about 1 minute, or until the butter is soft and spreadable.

3 After whipping the butter, line a baking sheet with parchment paper. Using a rubber spatula, spread the butter onto the parchment paper in a nice and even sheet that is about ¼ inch thick. If you are using a tool for texture, drag the tool across the surface of the butter. Place the butter in the freezer for about 20 minutes.

4 Fill a small container with hot water and place your Christmas cookie cutters into the water. Remove the hardened butter from the freezer and use the warmed cookie cutters to cut the butter into the desired shapes. Immediately transfer the butter to a board, garnish with the fresh herbs and pomegranate seeds, and serve with watermelon radishes, orange slices, and the Cranberry Relish.

ITALIAN BUTTER WITH ROSEMARY FOCACCIA

As beautiful as this board looks, it tastes even better. Bedazzled with Italian-inclined seasonings, this butter needs nothing more than a simple, delicious bread.

4 oz. unsalted butter, softened

¼ teaspoon kosher salt

Garlic Confit (see page 18), for garnish

Red pepper flakes, for garnish

Freshly cracked black pepper, for garnish

Dried basil, for garnish

Dried oregano, for garnish

Dried parsley, for garnish

Fresh basil, chopped, for garnish

Fresh parsley, chopped, for garnish

Fresh thyme, chopped, for garnish

Fresh rosemary, chopped, for garnish

Rosemary Focaccia (see page 50), for serving

1 Place the butter in the work bowl of a stand mixer fitted with the paddle attachment and add the salt.

2 Mix on medium-low for about 1 minute, or until the butter is soft and spreadable.

3 Spread the butter on a board in the desired manner, garnish with the Garlic Confit, red pepper flakes, pepper, dried herbs, and fresh herbs, and serve with the Rosemary Focaccia.

ROSEMARY FOCACCIA

1 Whisk the yeast and sugar into the water until they dissolve and set the mixture aside.

2 In the work bowl of a stand mixer fitted with the dough hook attachment, add the flour, salt, rosemary, and olive oil.

3 Once you see that the yeast is active—it will start to gently froth after about 5 minutes—add the yeast mixture to the work bowl and mix on low speed for about 7 minutes, until the dough is slightly tacky to the touch but releases from the side and bottom of the bowl.

4 Remove the dough and place it into a large bowl that has been lightly coated with olive oil. Loosely cover the bowl with plastic wrap and place it in a naturally warm place. Allow the dough to proof until it has doubled in size, about 2 hours.

5 Punch down the dough to release the gasses trapped inside and stretch it out in a 13 x 9–inch baking pan that has been coated with olive oil so that it covers the pan in an even layer. Press down on the dough with your fingers to make indents in it.

6 Cover the pan with plastic wrap and let the dough proof for another 1 to 2 hours, or until it has doubled in size.

7 When the bread is about 10 minutes from doubling in size, preheat the oven to 375°F.

8 Uncover the dough, being very gentle with the dough so as not to deflate it, and drizzle olive oil over the top.

9 Place the focaccia in the oven and bake for about 20 to 25 minutes, rotating the pan halfway through, until the top is a beautiful golden brown and the focaccia sounds hollow when you tap on it.

10 Remove the focaccia from the oven and let it cool completely before serving.

¾ tablespoon active
dry yeast

1 tablespoon sugar

5 oz. lukewarm water (90°F)

10 oz. bread flour

2 teaspoons kosher salt

2 tablespoons chopped
rosemary

2 tablespoons extra-virgin
olive oil, plus more
as needed

TRUFFLE BUTTER WITH CRACKERS

This decadent recipe is the perfect means of incorporating truffles without having to break the bank. Using both canned truffles and truffle oil, this butter is a great way to indulge in truffles even when they are not in season.

4 oz. unsalted butter, softened

¼ teaspoon kosher salt

2 tablespoons truffle oil, plus more for garnish

1 teaspoon soy sauce

1 teaspoon chopped canned truffles, plus more for garnish

Fresh thyme, for garnish

Crackers, for serving

1 Place the butter in the work bowl of a stand mixer fitted with the paddle attachment and add the salt, truffle oil, soy sauce, and truffle pieces.

2 Mix on medium-low for about 1 minute, or until all of the ingredients have evenly blended into the butter, and the butter is a smooth and airy mixture.

3 Use a rubber spatula to scrape down the side and bottom of the work bowl. Mix again at medium speed for another 15 to 30 seconds to ensure that all of the butter gets evenly incorporated.

4 Spread the butter on a board in the desired manner. Garnish with thyme, additional truffle oil, and additional truffles, and serve with crackers.

If you are really feeling lavish, feel free to top this butter board with some freshly shaved truffles and make it fit for royalty.

PESTO BUTTER WITH ROSEMARY FOCACCIA

This butter board, inspired by travels throughout Tuscany and Rome, packs tons of flavor and features three Italian treasures: pesto, focaccia, and Parmigiano-Reggiano. This board is a great one for summertime.

4 oz. unsalted butter, softened

¼ teaspoon kosher salt

2 oz. Pesto (see page 56)

Parmigiano-Reggiano cheese, for garnish

Rosemary Focaccia (see page 50), for serving

1 Place the butter in the work bowl of a stand mixer fitted with the paddle attachment and add the salt and Pesto.

2 Mix on medium-low for 2 to 3 minutes, or until all of the ingredients have evenly blended into the butter.

3 Use a rubber spatula to scrape down the side and bottom of the work bowl. Mix again at medium speed for another 15 to 30 seconds to ensure that all of the butter gets evenly incorporated.

4 Spread the butter on a board in the desired manner, garnish with chunks of Parmigiano-Reggiano, and serve with the Rosemary Focaccia.

PESTO

¼ cup pine nuts

½ cup fresh parsley

2 cups fresh basil

2 tablespoons fresh thyme

¼ cup fresh mint

½ cup grated Parmigiano-Reggiano cheese

5 cloves of Garlic Confit (see page 18)

Zest of 1 lemon

Salt, to taste

½ cup extra-virgin olive oil

1   Preheat the oven to 300°F and place the pine nuts on a baking sheet.

2   Pick all of the herbs so that only the leaves remain, making sure to keep them separate. You are going to blanch and shock half of the parsley and half of the basil.

3   Bring a pot of water to a boil. Fill a bowl with ice water. Add half of the parsley and basil to the boiling water and cook for about 30 seconds. After 30 seconds, strain the herbs from the boiling water and immediately dump them into the ice water to stop the cooking process. Once the herbs have cooled, squeeze out any excess water and set them aside.

4   Place the pine nuts in the oven and toast for about 6 minutes, until they are golden brown. Set them aside to cool.

5   Place all of the herbs into a blender or food processor. Add the pine nuts, Parmigiano-Reggiano, Garlic Confit, lemon zest, salt, and olive oil. Puree on a low speed until everything is chopped and mixed together but not completely smooth.

6   Season the pesto to taste and chill it in the refrigerator before serving.

CHOW CHOW BUTTER WITH CRACKERS

This simple to make yet complexly flavored butter board is the perfect spread to have ready for when you are doing last-minute entertaining. Simply whip up some butter, put out some crackers, and crack open a jar of chow chow that you've preserved, and your guests will think you put in much more effort than you did.

Chow chow, like most regional recipes in the United States, will vary greatly depending on who is making it and where they are from, ranging from roughly cut pickled vegetables to a cooked-down relish. One thing you can count on—it's a delicious medley of vegetables.

4 oz. unsalted butter, softened

¼ teaspoon kosher salt

Summer Vegetable Chow Chow (see page 60), for garnish

Fresh rosemary, chopped, for garnish

Fresh parsley, chopped, for garnish

Fresh thyme, for garnish

Crackers or bread, for serving

1 Place the butter in the work bowl of a stand mixer fitted with the paddle attachment and add the salt.

2 Mix on medium-low for about 1 minute, or until the butter is soft and spreadable.

3 Spread the butter on a board in the desired manner, garnish with the Summer Vegetable Chow Chow and fresh herbs, and serve with crackers or bread.

SUMMER VEGETABLE CHOW CHOW

1½ cups water

¾ cup rice vinegar

3 tablespoons kosher salt

½ cup sugar

1 yellow summer squash, diced

1 zucchini, diced

1 bell pepper, diced

4 teaspoons mustard seeds

1 tablespoon dried basil

¼ teaspoon red pepper flakes

1 Add the water, rice vinegar, salt, and sugar to a small saucepan and warm over medium heat, stirring occasionally until everything is dissolved and the mixture comes to a gentle simmer.

2 Place the vegetables, mustard seeds, basil, and red pepper flakes in a mason jar.

3 Pour the brine over the vegetables until they are entirely covered.

4 Put a lid on the container and store it in the refrigerator overnight until thoroughly chilled before serving. The chow chow will keep in the refrigerator for up to 1 month.

VEGAN BUTTER WITH PUFFED FORBIDDEN BLACK RICE & CRUDITÉS

Just because vegans don't eat butter doesn't mean they have to miss out on all the fun! This butter board, which is made using vegan butter made from plants, is topped with Puffed Forbidden Black Rice, which gives the butter a wonderful crunch, and is served with a medley of fresh vegetables to claim the title of our healthiest butter board.

Forbidden black rice, which gets its name from the fact that only the emperor was allowed to eat it in ancient China, can be puffed to create a crunchy morsel similar to crisped rice cereal. We use this tasty rice to add texture to lots of salads and spreads.

4 oz. Earth Balance Original Buttery Spread, softened

Puffed Forbidden Black Rice (see page 63), for garnish

Crudités, for serving

1 Spread the buttery spread on a board in the desired manner, garnish with the Puffed Forbidden Black Rice, and serve with crudités.

PUFFED FORBIDDEN BLACK RICE

2 cups canola oil

¼ cup uncooked forbidden black rice

¼ teaspoon kosher salt

1   In a 2-quart or larger saucepan, heat the canola oil until it reaches a temperature of 425°F. The rice will bubble rapidly and expand, so make sure that you do not add too much rice at once and that your pot is big enough to contain the expansion.

2   While the oil is heating, line a baking sheet with paper towels and set a fine-mesh strainer close to the pot of oil.

3   Once the oil has reached 425°F, carefully place half of your rice into the oil and allow the rice to cook for about 20 to 30 seconds, or until all of the rice kernels have become puffy. Strain the rice to remove it from the oil and place it on the baking sheet to drain. Repeat with the remaining rice.

4   Season the puffed rice with the salt and serve.

4 oz. unsalted butter, softened

2 oz. tomato paste

¼ teaspoon kosher salt

Extra-virgin olive oil, for garnish

Freshly cracked black pepper, for garnish

Red pepper flakes, for garnish

Fresh basil, chopped, for garnish

Fresh parsley, chopped, for garnish

Fresh rosemary, chopped, for garnish

Fresh thyme, for garnish

Garlic Confit (see page 18), for garnish

Balsamic vinegar, for garnish

Cherry tomatoes, halved, for serving

Bread or crackers, for serving

TOMATO BUTTER WITH BREAD & CHERRY TOMATOES

This board is the perfect way to celebrate the all-too-brief peak of tomato season. Using tomato paste helps cut through the richness of the butter and provides a strong tomato punch, resulting in a butter that pairs perfectly with any bread, and can also serve as the perfect butter to finish your favorite pasta or rice dishes with.

1   Place the butter in the work bowl of a stand mixer fitted with the paddle attachment and add the tomato paste and salt.

2   Mix on medium-low for about 2 minutes, or until all of the ingredients have evenly blended into the butter.

3   Use a rubber spatula to scrape down the side and bottom of the work bowl. Mix again at medium speed for another 15 to 30 seconds to ensure that all of the butter gets evenly incorporated.

4   Spread the butter on a board in the desired manner, garnish with olive oil, pepper, red pepper flakes, fresh herbs, Garlic Confit, and balsamic vinegar, and serve with cherry tomatoes and bread or crackers.

DILL, CAPER & CREAM CHEESE BUTTER WITH LOX & BAGEL CHIPS

Instead of putting out an assortment of bagels and cream cheeses the next time you have family in town, try pulling out this board and watch how excited everyone gets.

4 oz. cream cheese, softened

Zest of 1 lemon

½ teaspoon honey

1 tablespoon capers, plus more for garnish

¼ teaspoon kosher salt

2 oz. unsalted butter, softened and cut into small cubes

1 tablespoon chopped fresh dill, plus more for garnish

Everything bagel seasoning, for garnish

Gravlax, for serving

Bagel chips, for serving

1 Place the cream cheese in the work bowl of a stand mixer fitted with the paddle attachment and add the lemon zest, honey, capers, and salt.

2 Mix on medium-low for about 1 minute, or until all of the ingredients have evenly blended into the cream cheese.

3 Use a rubber spatula to scrape down the side and bottom of the work bowl. Mix again at medium speed for another 15 to 30 seconds to ensure that all of the cream cheese gets evenly incorporated.

4 Add the butter, 1 tablespoon at a time, allowing each addition to be incorporated before adding another portion of butter.

5 Add the dill and mix to incorporate.

6 Spread the butter on a board in the desired manner, garnish with additional dill and capers and everything bagel seasoning, and serve with gravlax and bagel chips.

SOY BUTTER WITH TEMPURA VEGETABLES

This board features a slightly salty Soy Butter with deep umami notes, a sweet-yet-spicy Chile Dipping Sauce, and crispy fried vegetables that have been coated in a delicate tempura batter.

4 oz. unsalted butter, softened

1 tablespoon soy sauce

Tempura Vegetables (see page 70), for serving

Chile Dipping Sauce (see page 71), for serving

1 Place the butter in the work bowl of a stand mixer fitted with the paddle attachment and add the soy sauce.

2 Mix on medium-low for about 2 minutes, or until the soy sauce has evenly blended into the butter.

3 Use a rubber spatula to scrape down the side and bottom of the work bowl. Mix again at medium speed for another 15 to 30 seconds to ensure that all of the butter gets evenly incorporated.

4 Spread the butter on a board in the desired manner. Serve with the Tempura Vegetables and Chile Dipping Sauce.

TEMPURA VEGETABLES

Canola oil, as needed

1 egg

7 oz. club soda, chilled

1 teaspoon baking powder

1 cup cake flour

3 cups chopped vegetables

Salt, to taste

1   Fill a heavy-bottomed pot with canola oil until it is at least 4 inches deep, and heat the oil until it reaches 325°F.

2   While the oil is coming up to temperature, prepare your tempura batter. Crack the egg into a bowl and whisk it to break up the yolk. Stream in the club soda and whisk to combine.

3   Combine the baking powder and flour and sift the mixture into the egg mixture. Whisk gently, using a fork, until the batter comes together. The batter should have a consistency similar to a slightly thin pancake batter. Do not overmix.

4   Chill the batter in the refrigerator while you wait for the oil to heat up.

5   Set up an assembly line to fry efficiently without making a mess: start with the vegetables to the left of the fryer, with the batter between the vegetables and the stove. On the right side of the stove, place a bowl with tongs or a slotted spoon, salt, and a plate or pan lined with paper towels. Season the vegetables with a liberal sprinkle of salt.

6   Using tongs, one at a time, take each piece of vegetable and submerge it in the batter so that it is completely coated, and then gently transfer it to the oil. Make sure to gently dip each piece of vegetable into the oil so it does not sink to the bottom and stick. Make sure to only fry 5 or 6 pieces at a time.

7   Let each piece fry for 2 ½ to 3 minutes, or until it is light golden brown and floating. You may need to flip each vegetable to ensure even browning.

8   Gently remove each vegetable from the fryer and place it in a bowl. Season with salt and transfer the fried vegetables to a paper towel–lined plate to drain. Let the oil come back to 325°F before adding each batch of vegetables and serve once they are all fried.

CHILE DIPPING SAUCE

1 cup sweet chile sauce

¼ cup hoisin sauce

2 tablespoons soy sauce

1½ teaspoons minced fresh ginger

1½ teaspoons minced lemongrass

1 garlic clove, grated

Zest and juice of 1 lime

Salt, to taste

1 Add the sweet chile sauce, hoisin sauce, and soy sauce to a bowl and whisk until everything is combined. Add the ginger and lemongrass.

2 Add the garlic, lime zest, and lime juice to the chile mixture and whisk to incorporate. Season with salt and serve.

RANCH BUTTER WITH CRUDITÉS & CRACKERS

We harnessed the tangy, fresh flavor of America's favorite dressing and turned it into a butter that serves as the perfect accompaniment for both fresh vegetables and crackers.

4 oz. unsalted butter, softened

¼ cup scallions, chopped

2 tablespoons chopped fresh chives

2 tablespoons Garlic Confit (see page 18)

¼ cup chopped fresh Italian parsley

Zest of 1 lemon

Juice of ½ lemon

3 dashes of Tabasco

3 dashes of Worcestershire sauce

2 tablespoons buttermilk

¼ teaspoon black pepper

½ teaspoon kosher salt

Crudités, for serving

Crackers, for serving

1 Place the butter in the work bowl of a stand mixer fitted with the paddle attachment and add all of the remaining ingredients, except for the crudités and crackers.

2 Mix on medium-low for about 2 minutes or until all of the ingredients have evenly blended into the butter.

3 Use a rubber spatula to scrape down the side and bottom of the work bowl. Mix again at medium speed for another 15 to 30 seconds to ensure that all of the butter gets evenly incorporated.

4 Spread the butter on a board in the desired manner and serve with crudités and crackers.

MISO BUTTER WITH SUGAR SNAP PEAS

The addition of white miso paste, which is a popular Japanese condiment made from fermented soybeans, gives butter a salty burst that is balanced with subtle umami notes. While we use this butter as a spread for fresh vegetables, it would also serve as a fantastic butter to finish proteins straight out of the oven.

4 oz. unsalted butter, softened

2 tablespoons white miso paste

Toasted sesame seeds, for garnish

Sugar snap peas, for serving

1 Place the butter in the work bowl of a stand mixer fitted with the paddle attachment and add the miso.

2 Mix on medium-low for about 1 minute or until the miso has evenly blended into the butter.

3 Use a rubber spatula to scrape down the side and bottom of the work bowl. Mix again at medium speed for another 15 to 30 seconds to ensure that all of the butter gets evenly incorporated.

4 Spread the butter on a board in the desired manner, garnish with toasted sesame seeds, and serve with sugar snap peas.

HUMMUS BUTTER WITH CRISPY CHICKPEAS & NAAN

This butter is essentially hummus that is enriched with butter by having it incorporated directly into the spread. The result is a rich butter-hummus hybrid that possesses the flavor of hummus with the smooth and creamy texture of butter.

These air-fried chickpeas are quick and easy to make and are a fantastic addition to any vegetarian dish you are looking to add some crunch to.

4 oz. Hummus (see page 78)

¼ teaspoon kosher salt

2 oz. unsalted butter, softened and diced

Paprika, for garnish

Extra-virgin olive oil, for garnish

Crispy Chickpeas (see page 79), for serving

Naan (see page 44), for serving

1 Place the Hummus in the work bowl of a stand mixer fitted with the whisk attachment and add the salt.

2 Whip the Hummus on medium-low for about 1 minute, or until it is light and airy.

3 Add 1 chunk of butter at a time and whip until the butter is fully incorporated before adding the next.

4 Spread the butter on a board in the desired manner, garnish with paprika and olive oil, and serve with the Crispy Chickpeas and Naan.

HUMMUS

1 (14.5 oz.) can of chickpeas, drained, liquid reserved

¼ cup extra-virgin olive oil, plus more as needed

2 shallots, julienned

1 tablespoon cumin

1½ teaspoons coriander

1 tablespoon Garlic Confit (see page 18)

¼ cup tahini paste

Zest and juice of 1½ lemons, plus more to taste

Salt, to taste

1 Place the chickpeas and reserved liquid in a large bowl and set the mixture aside.

2 Warm a large skillet over high heat for about 1 minute. Add about 1 teaspoon of olive oil and the shallots. Turn the heat down to medium-low and continue to cook the shallots, stirring occasionally, for about 5 minutes, or until they all begin to look golden and translucent, with subtle char on the ends.

3 Add about ⅓ cup of water to the pan to deglaze and continue cooking on medium-low heat until all of the liquid has evaporated and the shallots are a dark gold color and appear slightly translucent.

4 Turn the heat down to the lowest setting, add the cumin, coriander, and Garlic Confit, and stir to coat the shallots. Continue to cook, toasting the spices for 1 to 2 minutes.

5 Add the shallot mixture to the bowl with the chickpeas, deglazing the pan again if necessary to release any spices stuck to the pan.

6 Add the tahini, lemon zest, lemon juice, salt, and olive oil and toss everything together to combine.

7 Using a food processor, puree the mixture until it is smooth.

8 Season the hummus to taste with salt and lemon juice and chill before using.

CRISPY CHICKPEAS

1 (14.5 oz.) can of chickpeas, drained

1 tablespoon extra-virgin olive oil

½ teaspoon cumin

½ teaspoon kosher salt

Juice of ½ lemon

1   Preheat an air fryer to 375°F.

2   Transfer the chickpeas to a bowl. Add the olive oil, cumin, and salt and toss to coat.

3   Transfer the chickpeas to the air fryer and cook for about 15 to 20 minutes, or until the chickpeas are crispy.

4   Once the chickpeas are crispy, toss them with the lemon juice and serve immediately.

BUFFALO BUTTER WITH VEGGIES, BLUE CHEESE CRUMBLES & CRACKERS

Who doesn't love buffalo hot sauce? For this butter board, we added our favorite buffalo sauce, along with a bit of mayo, and topped it with some chopped scallions and blue cheese crumbles.

This butter is great to be served with carrot and celery sticks or even buffalo wings.

4 oz. unsalted butter, softened

2 oz. buffalo sauce

1 tablespoon mayonnaise

¼ teaspoon kosher salt

Blue cheese, crumbled, for garnish

Scallions, chopped, for garnish

Celery, chopped, for serving

Carrots, sliced, for serving

Crackers, for serving

1 Place the butter in the work bowl of a stand mixer fitted with the paddle attachment and add the buffalo sauce, mayonnaise, and salt.

2 Mix on medium-low for about 2 minutes, or until all of the ingredients have evenly blended into the butter.

3 Use a rubber spatula to scrape down the side and bottom of the work bowl. Mix again at medium speed for another 15 to 30 seconds to ensure that all of the butter gets evenly incorporated.

4 Spread the butter on a board in the desired manner, garnish with blue cheese crumbles and scallions, and serve with celery, carrots, and crackers.

CHIPOTLE BUTTER WITH BLISTERED SHISHITO PEPPERS & TORTILLA CHIPS

This board is all about varying forms of spice. As you enjoy, you will experience differing waves of heat, ranging from the deep, smoky chipotle heat to the acid-zing heat from the Tajín, to the carbon-scented, fresh heat from the Blistered Shishito Peppers. We crank up the spice of this butter with the addition of canned chipotle peppers. To balance the bitterness and brighten the flavor of the butter as a whole, we also add a splash of agave syrup. This butter makes a great spread or can be worked into hundreds of other recipes.

4 oz. unsalted butter, softened

2 oz. chipotle peppers in adobo

1 teaspoon agave nectar

¼ teaspoon kosher salt

Tajín, for garnish

Blistered Shishito Peppers (see page 84), for serving

Tortilla chips or chicharron, for serving

1 Place the butter in the work bowl of a stand mixer fitted with the paddle attachment and add the chipotle peppers, agave nectar, and salt.

2 Mix on medium-low for about 2 minutes, or until all of the ingredients have evenly blended into the butter.

3 Use a rubber spatula to scrape down the side and bottom of the work bowl. Mix again at medium speed for another 15 to 30 seconds to ensure that all of the butter gets evenly incorporated.

4 Spread the butter on a board in the desired manner, garnish with the Tajín, and serve with the Blistered Shishito Peppers and tortilla chips or chicharron.

BLISTERED SHISHITO PEPPERS

1 tablespoon canola oil

4 oz. shishito peppers

¼ teaspoon kosher salt

1   Warm a large cast-iron skillet over high heat for about 1 to 2 minutes, or until it is hot enough to steam a drop of water instantly on the surface.

2   Add the canola oil to the pan, followed by the shishito peppers—be careful, as the oil may spatter—placing the peppers in a single layer.

3   Cook the peppers for about 3 minutes without touching them so that the skin side in the pan becomes a dark brown and they start to blister.

4   Flip the peppers over and continue to cook on the other side for another 1 to 2 minutes.

5   After both sides of the peppers are dark and blistered, remove them from the pan and season them with the salt. Serve warm.

SMOKED BUTTER WITH DIPPED RADISHES & FRENCH BAGUETTE

This board is modeled after the traditional French bistro sandwich made with radishes, butter, and a baguette. We make things a little more exciting with the addition of lightly smoked butter, which the radishes will be dipped in to create a rich, smoky shell.

The key to successfully making smoked butter is subtlety. Smoke is one of those things that can get out of hand quickly and can easily throw off the balance of the whole board. If you are on the fence over whether to add more or less smoke, always go with less.

4 oz. unsalted butter, softened

¼ teaspoon kosher salt

2 to 3 radishes, sliced, for garnish

Coarse sea salt, for garnish

Fresh mint, chopped, for garnish

Extra-virgin olive oil, for garnish

Dipped Radishes (see page 87), for serving

1 baguette, sliced, for serving

1   Fill a smoker with your favorite wood chips and set it to either the lowest heat setting or no hotter than 200°F.

2   After the smoker has been smoking for about 20 minutes, pull the butter out of the refrigerator, place it in a heatproof container, and place it in the smoker. Place a small saucepan filled with ice on the rack directly below the butter.

3   Smoke the butter for about 15 minutes. The key is to slightly melt the butter but not get the butter so hot that it completely renders and separates.

4   Remove the butter from the smoker and gently stir in the kosher salt. Set half of the Smoked Butter aside and use it to make the Dipped Radishes.

5   Spread the remaining Smoked Butter on a board in the desired manner, garnish with radishes, coarse sea salt, fresh mint, and olive oil, and serve with the Dipped Radishes and baguette.

DIPPED RADISHES

6 to 8 small radishes

2 oz. Smoked Butter
(see page 85)

Coarse sea salt, to taste

1 Slice off the very bottom of each radish so that it will sit flat. Place them on a baking sheet lined with parchment paper and place them in the freezer for 5 to 10 minutes so that the surface of the radishes becomes very cold, but not so they freeze.

2 Either slightly heat or cool the Smoked Butter so that it is barely a liquid, between 84°F and 90°F.

3 Once the radishes are chilled, and the butter is liquid but not broken and separated, dip each radish into the butter and swirl to coat it all over. Once the radishes are fully coated in butter, place them back on the baking sheet and season with coarse sea salt. Chill the radishes in the refrigerator and let the butter shells harden. Serve slightly chilled.

1 tablespoon extra-virgin olive oil

2 small shallots, minced

¼ teaspoon kosher salt, plus more to taste

6 oz. red wine

4 oz. unsalted butter, softened

1 teaspoon chopped fresh rosemary, plus more for garnish

1 teaspoon fresh thyme, plus more for garnish

Pan-Seared Rib Eyes (see page 90), for serving

Herb-Roasted Potatoes (see page 91), for serving

BEURRE ROUGE BUTTER WITH PAN-SEARED RIB EYES & HERB-ROASTED POTATOES

Intended to be served as a full meal, this board features a red wine butter that is served with pan-seared beef rib eyes and roasted potatoes—perfect for a family.

This spread is made from a reduction of red wine, shallots, and fresh herbs that are slightly cooled and mixed into softened butter to create a uniform emulsion. The name "beurre rouge" comes from the classic French sauce that is made in a similar manner.

1   Warm a small pot over medium heat. Add the olive oil to the pot and allow it to heat up for roughly 30 seconds before adding the shallots.

2   Add 2 pinches of salt and sweat your shallots on medium-low heat for about 2 to 3 minutes, or until the shallots become slightly translucent.

3   Once the shallots become translucent, add the red wine and deglaze the pot. Turn the heat to medium and reduce the red wine for about 8 minutes, or until you are left with about 4 oz. of total volume, including the shallots. Remove the pot from the stove and let the mixture cool to room temperature, about 10 minutes.

4   Place the butter in the work bowl of a stand mixer fitted with the paddle attachment and mix on medium-low for about 1 minute, or until all of the butter has been evenly mixed and looks slightly airy.

5   Add the red wine reduction, along with the salt and fresh herbs, and mix at medium-high speed for about 1 to 2 minutes, or until all of the ingredients have been absorbed by the butter and you have one uniform compound butter.

6   Use a rubber spatula to scrape down the side and bottom of the work bowl. Mix again at medium speed for another 15 to 30 seconds to ensure that all of the butter gets evenly incorporated.

7   Spread the butter on a board in the desired manner, garnish with additional rosemary and thyme, and serve with the Pan-Seared Rib Eyes and Herb-Roasted Potatoes.

PAN-SEARED RIB EYES

3 (½ lb.) boneless beef rib eyes

Salt and pepper, to taste

1 tablespoon canola oil

1 tablespoon Beurre Rouge Butter (see page 89)

1 Twenty minutes prior to cooking the steaks, pull them out of the refrigerator and season them liberally with salt and pepper on both sides. Let the steaks sit at room temperature to allow the salt to penetrate through the steaks.

2 Warm a cast-iron skillet over high heat for about 30 seconds, then add the canola oil.

3 Pat the steaks dry on both sides with a paper towel, but do not remove the seasoning. Once the pan is hot and the oil is shimmering, carefully add the steaks into the pan and gently press them flat to ensure the entire bottom sides of the steaks are in contact with the pan. This will form that perfectly even sear.

4 Turn the heat down to medium and allow the steaks to cook for about 6 minutes. Resist the urge to move the steaks at this point.

5 Once you see the corners of the steaks that are face down in the pan turn a deep brown color, gently flip the steaks over.

6 After about 2 minutes, divide the Beurre Rouge Butter into three even portions and place about 1 teaspoon directly on top of each steak. Continue cooking for about 1 more minute, or until the steak is golden brown on both sides and cooked to your preferred level of doneness.

7 Remove the steaks from the pan and place them on a cutting board to rest before slicing, for about 10 minutes, then cut them against the grain and serve.

HERB-ROASTED POTATOES

1 lb. rainbow peewee potatoes

2 tablespoons extra-virgin olive oil

1 teaspoon kosher salt

¼ teaspoon paprika

1 tablespoon chopped fresh Italian parsley

1 tablespoon chopped fresh rosemary

1 teaspoon fresh thyme

1 Preheat the oven to 400°F and wash the potatoes.

2 Cut the potatoes into quarters, transfer them to a bowl, and toss them with the olive oil, salt, paprika, and fresh herbs.

3 Transfer the potatoes to a baking sheet, place them in the oven, and bake for 35 to 40 minutes, or until they are crispy on the outside and fully cooked on the inside.

4 Remove the potatoes from the oven and let them cool slightly. After they have cooled, taste one potato, adjust the seasoning if necessary, and serve.

SCALLION BUTTER WITH POTATO CHIPS

A good board to break out for St. Patrick's Day, because of the butter's subtle green color and because the Potato Chips go perfectly with a pint of Guinness.

4 oz. unsalted butter, softened

¼ teaspoon kosher salt

2 bunches of scallions, trimmed and chopped, plus more for garnish

Potato Chips (see page 94), for serving

1   Place the butter in a food processor along with the salt.

2   Turn the food processor to the lowest speed and chop the butter for about 30 seconds, or until it looks slightly whipped.

3   Add the scallions and continue to process the butter until it has turned slightly green and all of the butter has been mixed with the scallions. Use a rubber spatula to scrape down the side of the work bowl and bottom of the blade. Mix on low for another 15 to 30 seconds.

4   Spread the butter on a board in the desired manner, garnish with additional scallions, and serve with the Potato Chips.

POTATO CHIPS

1 russet potato, washed and cut into ⅛-inch-thick slices

2 cups canola oil

Salt, to taste

1   Place the potato in a bowl of ice water and let it soak for about 20 minutes. Place the canola oil in a pot and warm it to 325°F.

2   Drain the potato and pat the slices dry with paper towels.

3   When the oil has reached 325°F, begin frying the potatoes in batches that form a single layer in your pot. Cook for 3 to 4 minutes, or until the potatoes turn slightly golden brown, stirring occasionally.

4   Once the chips turn golden brown, remove the chips from the oil with a strainer and transfer them to a paper towel–lined baking sheet to drain. Season them generously with salt.

5   Continue until all of the chips are cooked, and then serve, or let them cool before storing in an airtight container.

POTATO CHIPS
SEE PAGE 94

4 oz. unsalted butter, softened

¼ teaspoon kosher salt

1 tablespoon chopped fresh sage

Roasted Cauliflower (see page 100), for serving

Cauliflower Popcorn (see page 101), for serving

BROWN BUTTER WITH ROASTED CAULIFLOWER & CAULIFLOWER POPCORN

For this butter board, we decided to showcase one of the most underrated butter sauces, brown butter. Brown butter is amazing because of the natural nutty flavor it acquires when you slow-cook butter and allow the milk solids to toast. Add in some fresh sage and cauliflower, and you've got a great gluten-free butter board that certainly doesn't skimp on the flavor!

1 Divide the butter into two equal portions and place half of it in a small saucepan. Place the other half, along with the salt, in the work bowl of a stand mixer fitted with the paddle attachment.

2 Place the saucepan over medium heat and melt the butter. Once the butter has melted, continue to cook over medium-low heat, swirling the butter in the pan occasionally to ensure it cooks evenly, for about 3 minutes, or until the bits in the butter begin to brown, and the butter begins to foam. You should start to smell a nutty aroma.

3 Once the butter has been browned, remove the pan from heat and continue to swirl to prevent it from burning. Add the sage, being careful of the butter spattering, and continue to swirl for about 30 seconds, or until the pot is no longer hot enough to cook the butter. Set the melted butter aside to cool, for about 5 minutes.

4 Add the remaining butter to the work bowl of a stand mixer fitted with the paddle attachment and mix on medium-low for about 15 seconds. Slowly stream the brown butter into the work bowl while the mixer is running at its lowest speed. Continue mixing for about 1 minute, or until all of the browned butter has evenly blended into the butter.

5 Use a rubber spatula to scrape down the side and bottom of the work bowl. Mix again at medium speed for another 15 to 30 seconds to ensure that all of the butter gets evenly incorporated.

6 Spread the butter on a board in the desired manner and serve with the Roasted Cauliflower and Cauliflower Popcorn.

ROASTED CAULIFLOWER

2 tablespoons extra-virgin olive oil

1 small head of cauliflower

½ teaspoon kosher salt

2 tablespoons unsalted butter, diced

2 tablespoons chopped fresh sage

Juice of ½ lemon

1 Preheat the oven to 425°F and coat a baking sheet with the olive oil.

2 Take your head of cauliflower and cut off the green root end along with any of the green leaves remaining. Discard the root end and the green leaves, but do not entirely cut out the root because you want to leave the heads of the cauliflower intact.

3 With the root end sitting flat on your cutting board, starting from left to right, slice the head into large cauliflower steaks that are between ¼ and ½ inch thick.

4 Arrange the cauliflower steaks on the baking sheet in a single layer. Reserve all of the mini cauliflower florets that break apart from the larger portions for the Cauliflower Popcorn (see opposite page).

5 Sprinkle the salt over the cauliflower and then disperse the small cubes of butter among the cauliflower, placing them directly on top of the steaks. Sprinkle the sage over the cauliflower steaks so that each one is evenly coated.

6 Place the cauliflower in the oven and roast it for about 20 minutes, or until the cauliflower is golden brown and tender.

7 Remove the cauliflower from the oven and drizzle the lemon juice over it. Carefully transfer the roasted cauliflower to the butter board, being careful not to let the cauliflower steaks fall apart.

CAULIFLOWER POPCORN

2 tablespoons unsalted butter

½ cup small cauliflower florets

¼ teaspoon kosher salt

1. Heat a large cast-iron skillet over medium heat for about 20 seconds and add the butter, followed by the cauliflower florets.

2. Cook the cauliflower in the butter, swirling the pan occasionally, for about 8 minutes, or until the cauliflower is a deep golden brown, crispy, and has absorbed all of the butter.

3. Season the cauliflower popcorn with the salt and serve.

SEASIDE BUTTER WITH CRAB CAKES

This board is an ode to the Maryland crab cake. With a butter that has all of the flavors and components of tartar sauce, crab cakes become a beautiful board component, making them a surefire crowd-pleaser.

4 oz. unsalted butter, softened

1 tablespoon mayonnaise

1 teaspoon Dijon mustard

2 tablespoons capers, drained, plus more for garnish

1 tablespoon shallots, minced

2 dashes of Tabasco

2 dashes of Worcestershire sauce

Zest and juice of ½ lemon

2 tablespoons chopped fresh chives

2 tablespoons chopped fresh dill, plus more for garnish

¼ teaspoon kosher salt

Old Bay Seasoning, for garnish

Maryland Crab Cakes (see page 104), for serving

1   Place the butter in the work bowl of a stand mixer fitted with the paddle attachment and add the remaining ingredients, except for the Old Bay seasoning and crab cakes.

2   Mix on medium-low for about 1 to 2 minutes, or until the ingredients have evenly blended into the butter.

3   Use a rubber spatula to scrape down the side and bottom of the work bowl. Mix again at medium speed for another 30 seconds to ensure that all of the butter gets evenly incorporated.

4   Spread the butter on a board in the desired manner. Garnish with additional dill and capers and the Old Bay seasoning, and serve with the crab cakes.

MARYLAND CRAB CAKES

1 lb. fresh crabmeat

Zest of 1 lemon

Juice of ½ lemon

½ teaspoon kosher salt

2 tablespoons chopped fresh chives

2 tablespoons chopped fresh Italian parsley

1 garlic clove, minced

1 teaspoon Old Bay seasoning

1 egg

3 tablespoons mayonnaise

1 tablespoon Dijon mustard

½ teaspoon Worcestershire sauce

½ teaspoon Tabasco

½ cup bread crumbs

Extra-virgin olive oil, as needed

1 Start by carefully picking through the crabmeat to ensure there are no shells. Gently transfer the crabmeat to a large bowl.

2 Add the lemon zest, lemon juice, salt, chives, parsley, garlic, and Old Bay seasoning to the crabmeat and gently toss to combine.

3 In a separate bowl, add the egg, mayonnaise, Dijon, Worcestershire, and Tabasco and whisk to combine.

4 Using a rubber spatula, add the dressing to the crabmeat and gently fold to combine. Be careful not to break up the crabmeat.

5 Fold in the bread crumbs and gently toss until all of the bread crumbs are evenly distributed. Sample the binding by squeezing a small amount of the mixture in your hand to see if there is excess moisture.

6 Portion the crab mixture into 12 portions that each weigh about 2 oz., and set them aside.

7 Warm a large nonstick or cast-iron skillet over medium heat. Add enough olive oil to barely coat the bottom of the pan and allow the oil to heat for about 30 seconds.

8 When the oil is hot, place 4 or 5 crab cakes into the pan, being very careful not to spatter yourself with hot oil. Gently press the top of each crab cake with a spatula to slightly flatten it. Turn the heat to medium-low and cook each crab cake for about 4 to 5 minutes, or until it turns golden brown.

9 Flip the crab cakes and continue to cook for another 3 to 4 minutes, or until both sides are golden brown and the internal temperature is 135°F. Repeat until all of the crab cakes are cooked, adding more oil if necessary, and serve immediately.

WHOLE-GRAIN MUSTARD BUTTER WITH LEMON & MINT PICKLES & BREAD

An ode to the godfather of boards—the charcuterie board. This sharp and tangy butter packs all of the punch you are used to getting from whole-grain mustard, but with a smooth and creamy mouthfeel. This butter is perfect for slathering on bread to eat by itself, or to use as a spread for a sandwich.

4 oz. unsalted butter, softened

3 tablespoons whole-grain mustard

¼ teaspoon kosher salt

Cured meats, for serving

Cheese, for serving

Bread, for serving

Lemon & Mint Pickles (see page 107), for serving

1 Place the butter in the work bowl of a stand mixer fitted with the paddle attachment and add the mustard and salt.

2 Mix on medium-low for about 2 to 3 minutes, or until all of the mustard has evenly blended into the butter.

3 Use a rubber spatula to scrape down the side and bottom of the work bowl. Mix again at medium speed for another 15 to 30 seconds to ensure that all of the butter gets evenly incorporated.

4 Spread the butter on a board in the desired manner and serve with a combination of your favorite cured meats, cheese, bread, and the Lemon & Mint Pickles.

LEMON & MINT PICKLES

1½ cups water

¾ cup rice vinegar

3 tablespoons kosher salt

½ cup sugar

1 large cucumber

Zest of 1 lemon

3 sprigs of fresh mint

1 Add the water, rice vinegar, salt, and sugar to a small saucepan and warm over medium heat, stirring occasionally, until everything is dissolved and the mixture comes to a weak simmer.

2 Slice the cucumber to your desired thickness. Put the sliced cucumber in two mason jars and add the lemon zest to the cucumber, along with the mint.

3 Pour the brine over the cucumber slices and gently stir, making sure they are submerged.

4 Seal the jars and chill them in the refrigerator overnight until fully chilled.

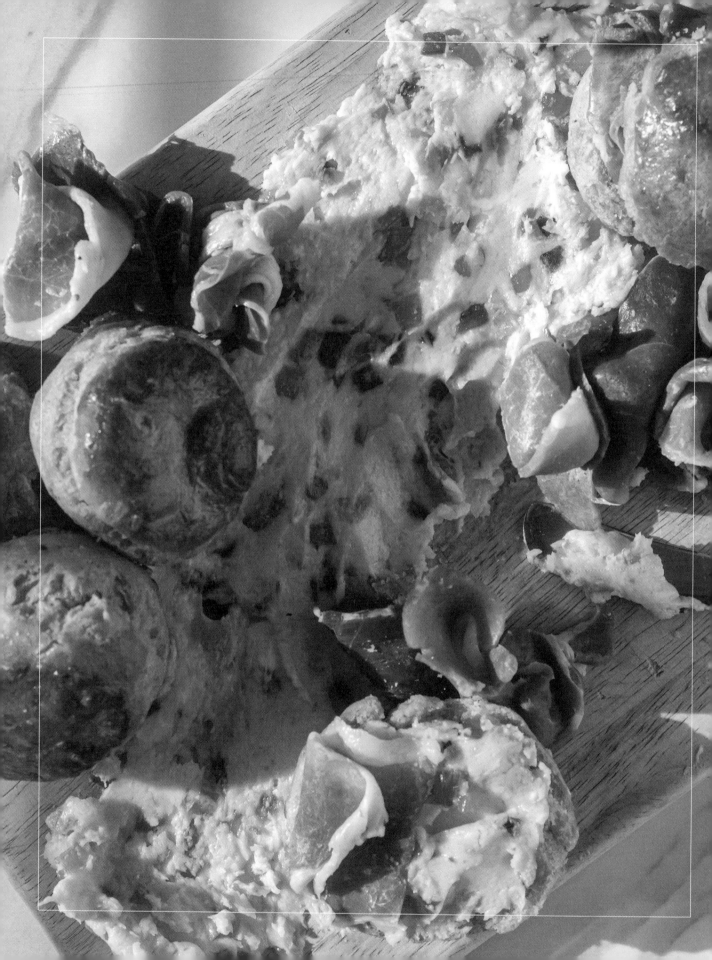

PEPPER JELLY BUTTER WITH COUNTRY HAM & BUTTERMILK BISCUITS

This board is essentially a deconstructed ham biscuit. The Pepper Jelly is folded into the butter to create a spread that would be wonderful to bring along on a picnic.

4 oz. unsalted butter, softened

¼ teaspoon kosher salt

2 oz. Pepper Jelly (see page 110)

8 slices of country ham, for serving

Buttermilk Biscuits, for serving (see page 112)

1   Place the butter in the work bowl of a stand mixer fitted with the paddle attachment and add the salt. Mix on medium-low for about 30 seconds.

2   Add the Pepper Jelly and continue to mix on medium-low until all of the jelly has blended into the butter.

3   Use a rubber spatula to scrape down the side and bottom of the work bowl. Mix again at medium speed for another 15 to 30 seconds to ensure that all of the butter gets evenly incorporated.

4   Spread the butter on a board in the desired manner and serve with the country ham and Buttermilk Biscuits.

PEPPER JELLY

Extra-virgin olive oil, as needed

½ cup diced red bell pepper

½ cup diced yellow bell pepper

½ cup diced orange bell pepper

⅓ cup diced red chile pepper

½ teaspoon kosher salt

½ cup sugar

Juice of ½ lemon

2 tablespoons apple cider vinegar

2 tablespoons pectin

1   Heat a 1-quart saucepan over medium-high heat for about 30 seconds.

2   Add a splash of olive oil and then the bell peppers and chile, followed by the salt. Mix all of the peppers together and cook over medium heat for about 5 minutes, or until the peppers have given off most of their moisture and the moisture has mostly evaporated.

3   Add the sugar and stir to dissolve it. Bring the mixture to a simmer and add the lemon juice and apple cider vinegar. Bring the mixture back to a gentle simmer and cook for about 15 minutes, stirring occasionally to ensure nothing sticks to the pan.

4   Whisk in the pectin and continue to simmer for another 3 to 4 minutes, until the mixture begins to thicken. Remove the jelly from the stove and let it cool completely before serving.

BUTTERMILK BISCUITS

1 Preheat the oven to 425°F.

2 Sift the flour, baking powder, baking soda, and fine sea salt together in a food processor and pulse to mix.

3 Add the butter and pulse a few times, until the butter breaks into pea-sized pieces. Do not overwork the butter.

4 Transfer the mixture to a large bowl, making a well in the middle as if you were making pasta dough.

5 Add the honey, then the buttermilk, to the well and gently mix to bring everything together. The dough will still be a little wet when fully incorporated. Do not overmix, or your biscuits will be dense and tough.

6 Dust your counter with flour and transfer the dough onto the counter.

7 Dust the top of the dough with more flour, and, using a rolling pin, gently roll the dough so that it is about ¼ inch thick. Fold half of the dough back over itself, so it is now about ½ inch thick, and gently roll the dough, pressing the two halves together.

8 Repeat the process one more time, but this time, gently work the dough. The dough does not have to be rolled to ¼ inch thick this time. It may be a little thicker.

9 After rolling out the dough, the dough should be about ¾ inch to 1 inch thick. At this point, cut your biscuits into the shapes you desire, about 2½ inches wide, and place them on a parchment-lined baking sheet. You can reroll any scraps of dough to make more biscuits, but be careful not overwork it.

10 Brush the biscuits with the egg, place them in the oven, and bake for 16 to 20 minutes, rotating the baking sheet halfway through the cooking time. The biscuits are finished when they are a deep golden brown on top and no longer doughy in the middle.

11 Remove the biscuits from the oven and either drizzle them with honey, brush with melted butter, or top with coarse sea salt.

2 cups all-purpose flour, plus more as needed

1 tablespoon baking powder

½ teaspoon baking soda

1½ teaspoons fine sea salt

6 tablespoons unsalted butter, chilled and diced

1 tablespoon honey, plus more for garnish, if desired

1 cup buttermilk

1 egg, beaten

Melted butter, for garnish (optional)

Coarse sea salt, for topping (optional)

SPICED HONEY BUTTER WITH CRACKERS

This butter is aesthetically pleasing and carries a unique flavor that shifts with every bite. With the various dried spices sprinkled sporadically across the board, this butter board truly is a dynamic experience for everyone involved.

4 oz. unsalted butter, softened

½ teaspoon honey

¼ teaspoon kosher salt

¼ teaspoon granulated onion

¼ teaspoon granulated garlic

¼ teaspoon dried thyme

¼ teaspoon dried basil

¼ teaspoon ground cumin

¼ teaspoon ground coriander

¼ teaspoon smoked paprika

2 pinches of cracked black pepper

2 pinches of roasted fennel seeds

2 pinches of red pepper flakes

2 pinches of ground mustard

2 pinches of pink Himalayan sea salt

Pinch of chili powder

Pinch of cayenne pepper

Crackers, for serving

1   Place the butter in the work bowl of a stand mixer fitted with the paddle attachment and add the honey and salt.

2   Mix on medium-low speed for about 1 minute, or until the butter looks light and airy.

3   Use a rubber spatula to scrape down the side and bottom of the work bowl. Mix again at medium speed for another 15 to 30 seconds to ensure that all of the butter gets evenly incorporated.

4   Spread the butter on a board in the desired manner.

5   Sprinkle all of the remaining ingredients, except for the crackers, over the butter in aesthetically pleasing patterns. Serve with crackers.

THE JACKSON POLLOCK BOARD

This board is an ode to the legendary artist Jackson Pollock, featuring variously colored butter "paints" that we drip onto our large canvas (a board). The result is not only dazzling aesthetically, but also a delightful culinary experience.

The key to creating and dripping the butters is heat control. You want your butters to be between 85°F and 90°F to achieve the proper consistency. If the butters become too warm, they will separate. If the butters are too cool, they will not drip, and you end up with big chunks of butter that miss the intent of the board. To manage the temperature properly, heat a small pot of water to about 140°F and set it aside. As you work with each butter, you can simply set the bowl containing the butter over the pot of water and whisk the butter until it thins out to the desired consistency.

Red Pepper Butter Paint
(see page 119)

Parsley Butter Paint
(see page 121)

Balsamic Butter Paint
(see page 122)

Whipped Butter Paint
(see page 123)

1 oz. Red Pepper Oil
(see page 118)

1 oz. Parsley Oil
(see page 120)

½ oz. balsamic vinegar

½ oz. extra-virgin olive oil

Bread or crackers,
for serving

1 Grab 4 paintbrushes, or use forks if you prefer.

2 To prepare the butter paints, heat a small pot of water to about 140°F and turn off the heat.

3 One by one, slowly heat the heatproof bowls containing each of the butter paints over the pot of warm water, whisking to gently liquefy the butter. Do not let the butters get above 90°F. Once the butters are close to 86°F, drip them onto a board, using a paintbrush or fork for each butter paint.

4 Drizzle the Red Pepper Oil, Parsley Oil, balsamic vinegar, and olive oil over the board to complete your canvas, and serve with bread or crackers.

RED PEPPER OIL

1 medium red bell pepper

2 oz. extra-virgin olive oil

2 pinches of kosher salt

1   Preheat the oven to 375°F and place your red bell pepper on a baking sheet.

2   Place the pepper in the oven and roast it for 45 minutes.

3   Remove the pepper from the oven, transfer it to a bowl, and cover the bowl with plastic wrap. Let the pepper steam for 10 minutes.

4   Remove the skin, stem, and seeds from the pepper and discard them.

5   Place the pepper in a blender, along with the olive oil and salt. Blend the mixture for about 1 minute, or until everything is smooth. Use immediately.

RED PEPPER BUTTER PAINT

2 oz. unsalted butter, softened

2 oz. Red Pepper Oil (see opposite page)

2 pinches of kosher salt

1   Place the butter in the work bowl of a stand mixer fitted with the whisk attachment and mix on medium-low for about 30 seconds, or until all of the butter looks light and airy.

2   Use a rubber spatula to scrape down the side and bottom of the work bowl and add the Red Pepper Oil and salt. Mix again at medium speed for another 1 to 2 minutes, or until all of the oil has emulsified.

3   Transfer the butter to a heatproof bowl and set it aside until you are ready to make the board.

PARSLEY OIL

1 bunch of fresh Italian parsley

2 pinches of kosher salt

3 oz. extra-virgin olive oil

1 Fill a medium saucepan with water and bring the water to a boil.

2 Fill a bowl with ice water and place it close to the stove.

3 Once the water comes to a boil, add the parsley and cook for about 20 seconds.

4 Remove the parsley from the boiling water and plunge it into the ice water. Keep it submerged until the parsley is fully chilled.

5 Remove the parsley from the ice water and squeeze out any excess water.

6 Cut the stems off the parsley, discard them, and transfer the parsley to a blender, along with the salt and olive oil. Puree for about 30 seconds, or until the mixture is smooth and uniform.

7 Strain the parsley oil through a fine-mesh sieve and use immediately.

PARSLEY BUTTER PAINT

2 oz. unsalted butter, softened

3 tablespoons Parsley Oil (see opposite page)

2 pinches of kosher salt

1 Place the butter in the work bowl of a stand mixer fitted with the whisk attachment and whip on medium-low for about 30 seconds, or until all of the butter looks light and airy.

2 Use a rubber spatula to scrape down the side and bottom of the work bowl and then add the Parsley Oil and salt. Mix again at medium speed for another 1 to 2 minutes, or until all of the oil has emulsified.

3 Transfer the butter to a heatproof bowl and set it aside until you are ready to make the board.

BALSAMIC BUTTER PAINT

2 oz. unsalted butter, softened

3 tablespoons balsamic glaze

2 pinches of kosher salt

1   Place the butter in the work bowl of a stand mixer fitted with the whisk attachment and whip on medium-low for about 30 seconds, or until all of the butter looks light and airy.

2   Use a rubber spatula to scrape down the side and bottom of the work bowl and then add the balsamic glaze and salt. Mix at medium speed for another 1 to 2 minutes, or until all of the glaze has emulsified.

3   Transfer the butter to a heatproof bowl and set it aside until you are ready to make the board.

WHIPPED BUTTER PAINT

2 oz. unsalted butter, softened

2 pinches of kosher salt

1   1. Place the butter in the work bowl of a stand mixer fitted with the whisk attachment and whip on medium-low for about 30 seconds, or until all of the butter looks light and airy.

2   Use a rubber spatula to scrape down the side and bottom of the work bowl and then add the salt. Mix again at medium speed for another 30 seconds.

3   Transfer the butter to a heatproof bowl and set it aside until you are ready to make the board.

SWEET

While most immediately think of savory
preparations to pair with butter, the truth is that
it is just as capable of sitting at the center of a
board that inclines itself toward sweetness. This
chapter celebrates this versatility, allowing you to
soothe any sweet craving with a desserty spread.

CINNAMON & HONEY BUTTER WITH BUTTER ROLLS & CANDIED ALMONDS

Honey amplifies butter's inherent sweetness, leaving plenty of room to accommodate cinnamon's unique spice. Matched with the soft, sweet rolls and decadent Candied Almonds, this board is a winner at any time of day.

For those who prefer another nut to almonds, feel free to swap it in here, as this foolproof technique will work with any nut.

4 oz. unsalted butter, softened

1 tablespoon honey, plus more for garnish

1 teaspoon cinnamon, plus more for garnish

½ teaspoon pure vanilla extract

¼ teaspoon kosher salt

Butter Rolls (see page 128), for serving

Candied Almonds (see page 130), for serving

1   Place the butter in the work bowl of a stand mixer fitted with the paddle attachment and add the honey, cinnamon, vanilla extract, and salt.

2   Mix on medium-low for about 1 minute, or until all of the ingredients have evenly blended into the butter.

3   Use a rubber spatula to scrape down the side and bottom of the work bowl. Turn the mixer back on at medium speed and continue to mix for 15 to 30 seconds to ensure that all of the butter gets evenly incorporated.

4   After all of the butter is mixed, spread it on the board in the desired manner and serve with the Butter Rolls and Candied Almonds.

YIELD: 25 ROLLS / ACTIVE TIME: 15 TO 20 MINUTES / TOTAL TIME: 4 HOURS

BUTTER ROLLS

1   Whisk the yeast into the water until it dissolves, then set the mixture aside.

2   In the work bowl of a stand mixer fitted with the dough hook attachment, add the flour, sugar, salt, butter, and egg. Mix until combined.

3   Once you see that the yeast is active—after about 5 minutes, it will start to gently froth—add the yeast mixture to the work bowl and mix on low speed, pulsing at first to make sure the flour doesn't shoot up the side of the bowl, for about 7 minutes. The dough will become smooth and should not stick to the side or bottom of the bowl.

4   Once the dough has been properly kneaded, place it in a bowl that has been lightly coated with butter. Cover the bowl with plastic wrap and place the dough somewhere warm to proof. Allow the dough to proof for about 2 hours, or until it has doubled in size.

5   Once the dough has doubled in size, remove the dough from the bowl, punch it down to release the gases, and shape it into small balls that are 1 oz. each. Roll each ball, applying subtle pressure onto the ball to ensure no pockets of air remain in the center. After rolling, place each ball into a 13 x 10-inch pan that has been coated with butter, so that the balls are a finger's length apart from one another. Cover the pan with plastic wrap and allow the rolls to proof in a warm place until they have tripled in size.

6   When the rolls are about 15 minutes away from tripling in size, preheat the oven to 375°F.

7   Place the rolls in the oven and bake the bread at 375°F for 15 to 20 minutes, rotating halfway through the baking process for even browning, or until the rolls are a deep golden brown on top.

8   Remove the pan from the oven and remove the rolls from the pan, then put them on racks to cool before serving.

1½ teaspoons active
dry yeast

7 oz. lukewarm water (90°F)

1 lb. bread flour

1¼ oz. sugar

¾ tablespoon kosher salt

2 oz. unsalted butter,
softened, plus more
as needed

1 large egg

CANDIED ALMONDS

1   Preheat the oven to 225°F and coat a baking sheet with a Silpat mat or parchment paper, then coat it with nonstick cooking spray. If you do not have a Silpat or parchment, heavily coat a baking sheet with nonstick cooking spray.

2   Separate the eggs and put the egg whites in the work bowl of a stand mixer fitted with the whip attachment. Make sure that the bowl is very clean and that none of the egg yolks get in with the egg whites.

3   Add the vanilla and cinnamon to the egg whites and begin mixing on low speed for about 10 seconds.

4   Once you have agitated the egg whites, turn the speed up to medium-high and continue to whip for 30 to 40 seconds, until the whites become frothy.

5   Slowly stream in the sugar while continuing to whip the egg whites on medium-high speed until the whites form soft peaks. They should have a smooth, glossy look.

6   Remove the bowl from the mixer, gently add the almonds to the bowl with the whipped egg whites, and softly fold in the almonds with a rubber spatula to coat evenly.

7   Spread the almonds on the baking sheet and sprinkle the salt evenly over the almonds. Place the pan in the oven and bake for 30 minutes.

8   Remove the pan from the oven and, using a rubber spatula, lift the almonds from the bottom of the pan and break them up. Once all of the large clumps are broken up, spread them back out in an even layer and continue to bake for another 30 minutes.

9   Remove the almonds from the oven and repeat the previous step to break them up once again. Continue to bake for another 30 minutes or until all of the almonds are completely dry.

10   Remove the pan from the oven and let it sit at room temperature for 15 minutes.

11   Remove the almonds from the baking sheet and store them in a dry, airtight container until ready to serve.

3 eggs

½ teaspoon pure
vanilla extract

1 teaspoon cinnamon

⅓ cup sugar

12 oz. unsalted almonds

1 teaspoon kosher salt

CANDIED ALMONDS
SEE PAGE 130

LEMON & GINGER BUTTER WITH STRAWBERRY RHUBARB JAM

Nothing says it's the height of spring quite like this board, which is bright and fruity, and carries just enough spice to keep your attention right where it should be.

4 oz. unsalted butter, softened

1 tablespoon honey

Zest of 1 lemon, plus more for garnish

2 teaspoons grated fresh ginger

¼ teaspoon kosher salt

3 tablespoons Strawberry Rhubarb Jam (see page 136), for serving

Toast, for serving

8 fresh strawberries, hulled and quartered, for serving

1 Place the butter in the work bowl of a stand mixer fitted with the paddle attachment and add the honey, lemon zest, ginger, and salt.

2 Mix on medium-low for about 1 minute, or until all of the ingredients have evenly blended into the butter.

3 Use a rubber spatula to scrape down the side and bottom of the work bowl. Mix again at medium speed for another 15 to 30 seconds to ensure that all of the butter gets evenly incorporated.

4 Spread the butter on a board in the desired manner. Garnish with additional lemon zest and serve with the jam, toast, and strawberries.

STRAWBERRY RHUBARB JAM

3 cups strawberries, hulled and quartered

3 cups diced rhubarb

1 tablespoon minced fresh ginger

2 cups sugar

Zest and juice of 2 lemons

2 pinches of kosher salt

1   Place the strawberries, rhubarb, and ginger in a heavy-bottomed pot.

2   Add the sugar, lemon zest, lemon juice, and salt and stir to combine.

3   Warm the mixture over medium-high heat, stirring occasionally, for 2 to 3 minutes, until the mixture reaches a gentle simmer.

4   Reduce the heat to low and continue to simmer, stirring frequently, for about 40 minutes, until the mixture starts to thicken and look syrupy.

5   Allow the jam to cool thoroughly before serving.

SPANISH CHOCOLATE BUTTER WITH CHURROS

Infused with bittersweet cocoa powder, accented with the sweet notes of cinnamon and vanilla, and finished with a hint of spice from cayenne pepper, this chocolate butter serves as the perfect parallel to the sauce that is traditionally served with churros.

The churro batter is a traditional one. Best of all, it can be prepared days ahead of time, stored in the refrigerator, and fried up at a moment's notice.

4 oz. unsalted butter, softened

1 tablespoon cocoa powder, plus more for garnish

½ teaspoon cinnamon

¼ teaspoon pure vanilla extract

1 teaspoon sugar

⅛ teaspoon cayenne pepper

¼ teaspoon kosher salt

Churros (see page 140), for serving

1 Place the butter in the work bowl of a stand mixer fitted with the paddle attachment and add the cocoa powder, cinnamon, vanilla extract, sugar, cayenne, and salt.

2 Paddle the mixture on medium-low for about 1 minute, or until all of the ingredients have evenly blended into the butter.

3 Use a rubber spatula to scrape down the side and bottom of the work bowl. Mix again at medium speed and continue to mix for another 15 to 30 seconds to ensure that all of the butter gets evenly incorporated.

4 Spread the butter on a board in the desired manner, garnish with additional cocoa powder, and serve with the Churros.

CHURROS

1 In a heavy-bottomed saucepan over medium-high heat, add the water, butter, vanilla, and 1 tablespoon of sugar and bring the mixture to a simmer. Sift the flour and salt together and set the mixture aside.

2 Turn the heat on the simmering water mixture down to low, add the flour mixture, and stir vigorously with a wooden spoon until a dough forms. Make sure that you break up all clumps of raw flour so that it forms a smooth dough. Continue to cook the dough on low heat for about 2 minutes, constantly stirring, until all of the bits of flour pull away from the bottom and side of the pot.

3 Set up your stand mixer with the paddle attachment and place the dough in the work bowl.

4 Turn the mixer to the lowest speed and add the eggs (including the yolk) one by one, being sure to fully incorporate each egg before adding another one.

5 Continue mixing on the lowest speed for about 4 minutes, or until the mixing bowl is no longer warm from the dough. Transfer the dough to a piping bag fitted with a star tip. Allow the batter to rest at room temperature for at least 30 minutes.

6 Place the remaining sugar and the cinnamon in a bowl and mix with a fork until the mixture is evenly combined. Set the mixture aside.

7 Add canola oil to a pot so that it is at least 3 inches deep, and heat the oil to 350°F.

8 Once the oil is hot, carefully pipe a strand that is between 4 and 6 inches long and snip the end closest to the tip so that the churro gently falls into the oil.

9 Allow the churro to cook in the oil for about 1 minute, and then gently flip the churro so that the opposite side is now submerged in the oil. Continue to cook for another 1 minute and 30 seconds, or until the entire churro is a nice golden brown.

10 Gently remove the churro from the oil, shake off the excess oil, and immediately place it in the cinnamon sugar mixture. Toss to coat the entire churro. Repeat, frying two or three churros at a time, depending on the size of the pot you are using, until all of the batter has been used. Serve warm.

1 cup water

5½ tablespoons unsalted butter

1 teaspoon pure vanilla extract

¼ cup plus 1 tablespoon sugar

1⅓ cups all-purpose flour

¼ teaspoon fine sea salt

3 eggs

1 egg yolk

1 tablespoon cinnamon

Canola oil, as needed

APPLE BUTTER WITH FRESH APPLES & RUSTIC WHITE BREAD

While it may not technically be a butter, apple butter is a delicious spread that definitely deserves to have a board built around it. So when that crisp, clean feeling enters the air and signals the arrival of fall, whip up this sweet, delicately spiced offering.

4 lbs. apples, peeled, cored, and chopped, plus more, sliced, for serving

1 teaspoon salt

2 tablespoons cinnamon

½ teaspoon freshly grated nutmeg

Juice of 2 lemons

1½ cups brown sugar

Rustic White Bread (see page 144), for serving

1 Preheat the oven to 250°F.

2 Place the apples in a large bowl and season with the salt, cinnamon, nutmeg, and lemon juice, then add the brown sugar and toss to distribute evenly.

3 Add the apple mixture to a large pan and wrap the top with plastic wrap, then aluminum foil. Make sure the plastic wrap is not hanging down lower than the foil.

4 Put the pan into the oven and bake for about 1½ hours.

5 After 1½ hours, take the pan out of the oven, pull off the plastic-and-aluminum foil layer, being careful to avoid the steam, and mix the apples to distribute the liquid.

6 Replace the plastic and aluminum foil, place the pan back in the oven, and continue baking for another 2 hours.

7 Remove the pan from the oven and let it cool at room temperature for about 20 minutes before pureeing the apples into a smooth mixture using a blender or food processor.

8 Taste the apple butter and adjust the seasoning to your liking before chilling in the refrigerator. Spread the butter on a board in the desired manner and serve with the Rustic White Bread.

RUSTIC WHITE BREAD

1½ teaspoons instant yeast

7 oz. lukewarm water (90°F)

1 lb. bread flour

1½ oz. sugar

¾ tablespoon kosher salt

2 oz. unsalted butter, softened, plus more as needed

1 large egg

1   Whisk the yeast into the water until it dissolves, and set it aside.

2   In the work bowl of a stand mixer fitted with the dough hook attachment, add the flour, sugar, salt, butter, and egg.

3   Add the yeast-water mixture to the mixer and mix the ingredients on low speed, pulsing at first to make sure the flour doesn't shoot up the side of the bowl, for about 7 minutes. The dough will become smooth and should not stick to the side or bottom of the bowl.

4   Place the dough in a bowl that has been lightly greased with butter. Wrap the bowl with plastic, place the dough somewhere warm to proof, and allow the dough to proof for about 2 hours, or until it has doubled in size.

5   Remove the dough from the bowl, punch it down to release the gasses, shape it into loaves that are about 1½ lbs. each, and roll them to fit into your desired pans. The pans should be large enough for the bread to triple in size.

6   Lightly grease your pans with butter, place the loaves inside them, wrap them loosely with plastic wrap, and put them in your proofing area, where they will triple in size.

7   When the dough is about 15 minutes away from reaching the tops of the pans, preheat the oven to 350°F.

8   Remove the plastic from the bread and bake the bread at 350°F for 15 to 20 minutes, rotating halfway for even browning, or until it is a deep golden brown and feels hollow when tapped.

9   Remove the bread from the pans and put it on racks to cool until ready to serve.

MAPLE BUTTER WITH LEMON RICOTTA PANCAKES & LEMON CURD

This board can serve as the ultimate breakfast in bed—
maple butter, pancakes, and lemon curd.

Lemon curd, which was initially called lemon cheese due to the fact
that the acidity from the lemon juice was used to separate the curds from the
whey of cream, can be used for many things. You can eat it by itself, spread it on
toast like you would jam, bake it into pastries such as lemon bars or Danish,
use it to make pies, and even top pancakes with it, as we do here.

Maple Butter (see page 151)

Fresh blueberries,
for garnish

Lemon Curd (see page 150),
for serving

Lemon Ricotta Pancakes
(see page 148), for serving

1 Spread the butter on a board in the desired manner,
garnish with fresh blueberries, and serve with the Lemon
Curd and Lemon Ricotta Pancakes.

LEMON RICOTTA PANCAKES

1 egg

Zest of 1 lemon

2 tablespoons sugar

1 tablespoon unsalted butter, melted

⅔ cup all-purpose flour

½ teaspoon baking soda

1 teaspoon baking powder

¼ teaspoon kosher salt

½ cup buttermilk

⅓ cup whole-milk ricotta cheese

1 Crack the egg into a bowl and add the lemon zest. Whisk to combine.

2 While whisking, stream in the sugar until all of the sugar is incorporated.

3 Stream in the melted butter while whisking until everything is incorporated.

4 Sift the flour, baking soda, baking powder, and salt into a separate bowl and set the mixture aside.

5 Slowly add the buttermilk to the egg mixture while whisking.

6 Once all of the buttermilk is fully mixed into the eggs, add the flour mixture and gently whisk until everything is incorporated.

7 Gently fold the ricotta into the batter, using a rubber spatula, until the ricotta is evenly distributed.

8 Place a nonstick skillet on the stove and warm it over medium-high heat for about 20 seconds. You want the pan to be hot but not smoking.

9 Coat the pan with nonstick cooking spray. Add about 1 oz. of batter to the pan and turn the heat down to medium-low. Cook the batter in the pan for about 3 minutes, or until the edges of the pancake turn golden brown.

10 Flip the pancake and continue to cook for another 2 to 3 minutes, or until the bottom side is also golden brown and the pancake is cooked all the way through. If you are in doubt, stick a toothpick into the center and pull it out. If the toothpick comes out clean, then it is fully cooked. Repeat until all of the pancakes are cooked and serve immediately.

LEMON CURD

3 eggs

2 egg yolks

½ lb. sugar

4 oz. unsalted butter, diced

Zest of 3 lemons, plus more to taste

3 oz. fresh lemon juice

Salt, to taste

1　Crack the eggs into a stainless-steel bowl that is large enough to sit comfortably on top of a pot that you can fill a quarter of the way with water to create a double boiler.

2　Fill the pot a quarter of the way with water, put it on the stove, and bring the water to a boil.

3　Add the remaining ingredients to the bowl and whisk to combine.

4　Once the water begins to boil, turn it down to a slow simmer and place the bowl on top of the pot to make a double boiler. The steam from the water in the pot below will slowly and gently cook the eggs, which will cause them to thicken slowly as opposed to scrambling. Whisk the mixture constantly, occasionally stopping to scrape down the side of the bowl with a rubber spatula, for about 10 to 15 minutes, or until the mixture reaches 170°F and thickens slightly.

5　Carefully remove the bowl from heat, transfer the lemon curd to another container, and chill it in the refrigerator. If you see little white clumps in your curd, this means it cooked too quickly and some of the eggs curdled. Simply push the curd before chilling. If you taste the curd once it is strained and it is missing some of that bright lemon pop, feel free to add some more lemon zest. Chill for at least 1 hour before serving.

MAPLE BUTTER WITH FRENCH TOAST & BACON

This slightly sweet butter will pair perfectly with a number of items, but it is at its best when served with anything that you would typically drizzle maple syrup over—such as the French Toast on this board.

4 oz. unsalted butter, softened

2 tablespoons pure maple syrup, plus more for garnish

¼ teaspoon kosher salt

Bacon, cooked, for serving

French Toast (see page 153), for serving

1   Place the butter in the work bowl of a stand mixer fitted with the paddle attachment and add the maple syrup and salt.

2   Mix on medium-low for about 1 minute or until all of the ingredients have evenly blended into the butter.

3   Use a rubber spatula to scrape down the side and bottom of the work bowl. Mix again at medium speed for another 15 to 30 seconds to ensure that all of the butter gets evenly incorporated.

4   Spread the butter on a board in the desired manner, drizzle additional maple syrup over it, and serve with bacon and the French Toast.

FRENCH TOAST

4 eggs

1 cup heavy cream

¼ teaspoon freshly grated nutmeg

½ teaspoon cinnamon

½ teaspoon pure vanilla extract

½ cup sugar

¼ teaspoon kosher salt

1 loaf of bread (we use brioche or challah), cut into ¾-inch-thick slices

Unsalted butter, as needed

1   Whisk the eggs together in a bowl to break them up, and slowly add the heavy cream, whisking constantly. Continue whisking until everything is fully incorporated.

2   Add the remaining ingredients, except for the bread and butter, and whisk everything together.

3   Submerge the bread in the egg mixture until the center of the bread has absorbed the batter, about 5 minutes.

4   Heat a large nonstick pan over medium-high heat.

5   Add a slice of butter to the pan and allow it to melt. Turn the heat down to medium-low.

6   Adding one piece of soaked French toast at a time, cook until the corners start to turn a deep golden brown, about 4 minutes per side.

7   Once both sides are a deep golden brown, the center should be soft but not runny, with a custard-like texture; that is when the French toast is fully cooked. Repeat with the remaining slices of bread, adding more butter to the pan as needed.

MARSHMALLOW BUTTER WITH GRAHAM CRACKERS & CHOCOLATE

Try bringing this s'more-styled board to your next bonfire.
The marshmallow butter is not butter per se, but a refined version
of the Marshmallow Fluff we all loved in our childhoods.

2 egg whites

4 oz. sugar

2 oz. water

Graham Crackers (see page 156), for serving

Chocolate, for serving

1   Add the egg whites to the work bowl of a stand mixer fitted with the whip attachment and whip on the lowest speed setting.

2   While whipping, add the sugar and water to a small saucepan and warm over medium heat, stirring to dissolve the sugar. Bring the syrup to a steady simmer and simmer the syrup until it reaches 235°F, about 6 minutes.

3   Adjust the mixer's speed to medium and continue to whip the egg whites until they reach soft peaks. With the mixer running at medium speed, slowly add the cooked syrup in a thin stream to the egg whites until all of the syrup is incorporated. When you add the syrup to the mixing bowl, the bowl will become hot. Keep whipping the egg whites on low speed until the bowl has cooled back down to room temperature, about 10 minutes, and the peaks become stiff and glossy.

4   Using a rubber spatula, remove the meringue from the bowl, spread it on a board in the desired manner, and serve with the Graham Crackers and chocolate.

GRAHAM CRACKERS

1 Add the butter, vanilla extract, and honey to the work bowl of a stand mixer fitted with the paddle attachment and begin mixing on low speed.

2 Slowly stream in the sugars and continue mixing until the mixture becomes light and airy, about 2 minutes.

3 Meanwhile, measure and sift the flours, salt, baking soda, and cinnamon into a bowl.

4 Turn the mixer off and add one-third of the flour mixture to the butter mixture. Mix slowly at the lowest speed to combine.

5 Scrape down the side and bottom of the work bowl to ensure it's all mixed, and add another one-third of the flour mixture. Repeat until all of the flour mixture has been incorporated, being careful not to overmix.

6 Remove the dough from the mixing bowl and tightly wrap it with plastic wrap. Refrigerate it for 30 minutes to 1 hour.

7 Remove the dough from the plastic wrap and place it on a lightly floured counter.

8 Preheat the oven to 350°F and coat a baking sheet with nonstick cooking spray.

9 Using a rolling pin, place the dough on a flour-dusted work surface and roll it out to about ⅛ inch thick. Using a square cookie cutter, or a pizza cutter, cut the dough into shapes that are 3-inch squares.

10 Using a pastry docker or fork, poke holes into each cracker and place them on the baking sheet. Bake for 12 to 15 minutes, or until the graham crackers are crisp and golden brown.

11 Remove the graham crackers from the oven, transfer them to cooling racks, and let them cool completely before serving.

12 oz. unsalted butter, softened

½ teaspoon pure vanilla extract

2 tablespoons honey

4.9 oz. brown sugar

4 oz. sugar

12.3 oz. all-purpose flour, plus more as needed

5.3 oz. whole wheat flour

¾ teaspoon fine sea salt

1 teaspoon baking soda

1 teaspoon cinnamon

GRAHAM CRACKERS
SEE PAGE 156

ORANGE & CLOVE BUTTER WITH CRANBERRY RELISH

As we mentioned, the Orange & Clove Butter is wonderful around the holidays, as this Thankgiving-themed board shows. Break this one out early in the day to get everyone excited for the delights to come, and serve any leftover Cranberry Relish in place of the canned, gelatinous cranberry sauce that is traditional.

Orange & Clove Butter
(see page 25)

Fresh thyme, for garnish

Bread or crackers,
for serving

Cranberry Relish (see page
162), for serving

1 Spread the butter on a board in the desired manner, garnish with thyme, and serve with bread and the Cranberry Relish.

CRANBERRY RELISH

1 lb. fresh or frozen cranberries

½ lb. dried cranberries

1 cup orange juice

Zest of 1 orange

Zest and juice of 1 lemon

2 cinnamon sticks

1 cup sugar

2 pinches of fine sea salt

1 Place all of the ingredients in a medium saucepan and bring to a simmer.

2 Turn the heat down and continue to simmer on low heat for about 15 minutes, until the cranberries explode and release some of their liquid.

3 Turn off the heat and allow the relish to cool and thicken before serving.

COCOA BUTTER WITH STRAWBERRIES

Break out this board on Valentine's Day to show your loved one just how much you care about them.

4 oz. unsalted butter, softened

1 tablespoon cocoa powder

¼ teaspoon pure vanilla extract

1 teaspoon sugar

¼ teaspoon kosher salt

Pomegranate seeds, for garnish

Shaved chocolate, for garnish

Rose petals, for garnish

1 lb. strawberries, hulled, for serving

1 Place the butter in the work bowl of a stand mixer fitted with the paddle attachment and add the cocoa powder, vanilla, sugar, and salt.

2 Mix on medium-low for about 1 minute, or until all of the ingredients have evenly blended into the butter.

3 Use a rubber spatula to scrape down the side and bottom of the work bowl. Mix again at medium speed for another 15 to 30 seconds to ensure that all of the butter gets evenly incorporated.

4 Spread the butter on a board in the desired manner, garnish with pomegranate seeds, shaved chocolate, and rose petals and serve with the strawberries.

COCOA BUTTER WITH PUMPKIN BREAD, ROASTED PEANUTS & SALTED CARAMEL

Bypass the candy this Halloween and bring this board to your next Halloween party: it's essentially a pumpkin-spiced latte meets a Snickers candy bar! As with any holiday party board, feel free to get creative and use your own spooky decorations.

Also, don't be intimidated by the homemade caramel—this is a not-so-temperamental recipe featuring corn syrup, which helps to stabilize the crystallization process while cooking the sugar.

Cocoa Butter (see page 165)

Pumpkin Bread (see page 168), for serving

Roasted peanuts, for serving

Salted Caramel (see page 170), for serving

1 Spread the butter on a board in the desired manner and serve with the Pumpkin Bread, peanuts, and Salted Caramel.

PUMPKIN BREAD

1 cup canola oil, plus more
as needed

3 eggs

3 cups brown sugar

1 teaspoon pure
vanilla extract

3 cups all-purpose flour

½ teaspoon baking powder

1 teaspoon baking soda

1 teaspoon fine sea salt

1 teaspoon cinnamon

1 tablespoon pumpkin spice

1 lb. pumpkin puree

1   Preheat the oven to 350°F and coat two 9 x 5–inch loaf
    pans with canola oil.

2   In the work bowl of a stand mixer fitted with the whisk
    attachment, add the eggs, brown sugar, and vanilla and
    mix on medium speed for about 3 to 4 minutes, or until the
    mixture looks pale and airy.

3   While the eggs and sugar are creaming, measure and sift
    the flour, baking powder, baking soda, salt, cinnamon, and
    pumpkin spice into a bowl and set the mixture aside.

4   Add the pumpkin puree to the work bowl and mix until
    fully incorporated. Stop the mixer halfway through
    incorporating the pumpkin and scrape down the side and
    bottom of the work bowl to ensure everything is fully mixed.

5   Slowly stream in the canola oil with the mixer running.

6   Add the flour mixture, little by little, into the pumpkin
    mixture and slowly mix to incorporate. Remove the bowl
    from the stand mixer and scrape down the work bowl to
    ensure everything is fully mixed. Do not mix more than
    what is necessary to incorporate the ingredients.

7   Divide the batter between the loaf pans, place them in the
    oven, and bake for about 50 minutes, or until a toothpick
    inserted into the middle of the loaves comes out clean.

8   Remove the loaves from the oven and let them cool in the
    pans for 5 to 10 minutes before transferring them to cooling
    racks. Let the loaves cool completely before serving.

SALTED CARAMEL

1 cup heavy cream

1½ teaspoons fine sea salt

1 cup sugar

½ cup corn syrup

1 Add the heavy cream and salt to a pot and heat over medium-low heat.

2 Bring the mixture to a gentle simmer, turn off the heat, and set aside.

3 Add the sugar and corn syrup to a separate, large pot and heat over medium-high heat, stirring to combine the ingredients.

4 Bring the mixture to a gentle boil, occasionally stirring, and cook for about 4 minutes.

5 Turn the heat down to medium and continue to cook at a steady simmer for about 8 minutes, stirring constantly. The sugars will start to caramelize and will gradually turn a light brown color.

6 Turn off the heat and continue to stir for at least 2 minutes, or until the mixture is no longer giving off steam. You don't want the sugar to burn.

7 Add the cream mixture carefully, little by little, about ¼ cup at a time, to the cooked sugar mixture, stirring carefully after each pour to incorporate. Use immediately.

CREAM CHEESE BUTTERCREAM WITH CARROT CAKE

Keep the frosting to the side and allow everyone to use as much as they want, providing the ultimate carrot cake experience.

4 oz. cream cheese, softened and diced

1 teaspoon pure vanilla extract

½ teaspoon cinnamon

¼ teaspoon kosher salt

2 oz. unsalted butter, softened and diced

½ cup confectioners' sugar

Carrot Cake (see page 174), for serving

1 Place the cream cheese in the work bowl of a stand mixer fitted with the paddle attachment, then add the vanilla, cinnamon, and salt and mix on medium-low speed for about 3 to 5 minutes.

2 Scrape down the side and bottom of the work bowl. Continue to mix for 1 minute at medium speed to ensure all of the cream cheese is evenly mixed.

3 Add the butter, one piece at a time, making sure each piece is completely mixed into the cream cheese before adding another.

4 With the mixer running on low, add the confectioners' sugar in a slow stream. Mix on low speed until everything comes together.

5 Spread the buttercream on a board in the desired manner and serve with the Carrot Cake.

CARROT CAKE

2 eggs

2 teaspoons pure vanilla extract

¾ cup sugar

1 cup all-purpose flour

¾ teaspoon baking powder

½ teaspoon baking soda

1 teaspoon cinnamon

¼ teaspoon fine sea salt

½ cup canola oil

1¼ cups peeled and grated carrots

½ cup raisins

½ cup chopped pecans

1   Preheat the oven to 350°F. Crack the eggs into the work bowl of a stand mixer fitted with the whisk attachment, add the vanilla extract, and start mixing on medium speed.

2   With the mixer running, stream in the sugar and continue to mix for about 4 to 5 minutes, or until the egg mixture becomes light and airy.

3   Meanwhile, sift the flour, baking powder, baking soda, cinnamon, and salt into a separate bowl and set the mixture aside.

4   With the mixer running, stream the canola oil into the work bowl and continue mixing until everything is incorporated.

5   Turn the mixer off, add about one-third of the flour mixture, and mix on low until incorporated.

6   Scrape down the side and bottom of the work bowl, add another one-third of the flour mixture, and mix on low again. Repeat with the remaining flour mixture, being careful not to overmix.

7   Remove the work bowl from the mixer. Using a rubber spatula, add the carrots, raisins, and pecans and gently fold them into the batter, scraping down the side and bottom of the work bowl.

8   Pour the batter into a round 9-inch cake pan and place the cake in the oven. Bake for about 40 minutes, or until you can insert a toothpick into the center of the cake without any batter sticking to it.

9   Remove the cake from the oven and let it cool for about 30 minutes before breaking it up for the butter board.

BROWN SUGAR BUTTER WITH HUSH PUPPIES & HONEY

This board is inspired by the heart of the Lowcountry, Charleston, South Carolina, and features one of its most popular treats, Hush Puppies, beside a slightly sweetened butter that can work at any time of day.

4 oz. unsalted butter, softened

2 tablespoons brown sugar

½ teaspoon kosher salt

Honey, for garnish

Hush Puppies (see page 178), for serving

1 Place the butter in the work bowl of a stand mixer fitted with the paddle attachment and add the brown sugar and salt.

2 Mix on medium-low for about 1 minute, or until all of the ingredients have evenly blended into the butter.

3 Use a rubber spatula to scrape down the side and bottom of the work bowl. Mix again at medium speed for another 15 to 30 seconds to ensure that all of the butter gets evenly incorporated.

4 Spread the butter on a board in the desired manner, garnish with honey, and serve with the Hush Puppies.

HUSH PUPPIES

Canola oil, as needed

1 egg

¼ cup sour cream

¼ cup buttermilk

Zest and juice of ½ lemon

1 teaspoon honey, plus more
for topping

3 dashes of Worcestershire sauce

3 dashes of Tabasco

1 teaspoon sugar

½ cup all-purpose flour

½ cup cornmeal

1 teaspoon paprika

2 teaspoons kosher salt, plus
more to taste

½ teaspoon black pepper

1 teaspoon baking powder

½ teaspoon baking soda

2 garlic cloves, chopped

1 tablespoon chopped fresh
Italian parsley

1 tablespoon chopped fresh chives

½ cup chopped scallions

1 Fill a heavy-bottomed pot with canola oil until it is
at least 4 inches deep and heat the oil until it
reaches 325°F.

2 While the oil is coming up to temperature, prepare
your batter. Crack the egg into a bowl and whisk it
to break up the yolk, then add the sour cream and
buttermilk and whisk to incorporate.

3 Add the lemon zest, lemon juice, honey,
Worcestershire, Tabasco, and sugar and whisk
to incorporate.

4 Combine the flour, cornmeal, paprika, salt, pepper,
baking powder, and baking soda in a separate bowl
and then add the mixture to the egg mixture. Stir
gently to break up all of the clumps and to combine.

5 Once the batter is smooth and has no dry spots, gently
fold in the garlic, parsley, chives, and scallions. The
batter should look slightly thicker than cornbread batter.

6 Working in batches of 4 to 6, gently drop heaping
tablespoons of batter into the oil. After about 2
minutes, gently tap on one side of each hush puppy to
flip it upside down so that the other side fries in the oil.
After another 2 minutes, all hush puppies should be a
beautiful golden brown on each side.

7 Remove the fried hush puppies from the oil, season with
salt, and drizzle some honey over them before serving.

BROWN SUGAR & CINNAMON BUTTER WITH BANANA NUT BREAD

This board features one of the great breakfast breads: banana. Made with walnuts, cinnamon, and vanilla, it pairs perfectly with the Brown Sugar & Cinnamon Butter, and toasted walnuts supply added crunch.

4 oz. unsalted butter, softened

2 tablespoons brown sugar

½ teaspoon cinnamon

½ teaspoon kosher salt

Banana Nut Bread (see page 182), for serving

1 banana, sliced, for serving

Toasted walnuts, for serving

1   Place the butter in a stand mixer fitted with the paddle attachment and add the brown sugar, cinnamon, and salt.

2   Mix on medium-low for about 1 minute, or until all of the ingredients have evenly blended into the butter.

3   Use a rubber spatula to scrape down the side and bottom of the work bowl. Mix again at medium speed for another 15 to 30 seconds to ensure that all of the butter gets evenly incorporated.

4   Spread the butter on a board in the desired manner and serve with the Banana Nut Bread, slices of banana, and toasted walnuts.

BANANA NUT BREAD

1   Preheat the oven to 350°F. Coat 2 loaf pans with nonstick cooking spray and dust them with flour, tapping out the excess.

2   Place the walnuts on a baking sheet, place them in the oven, and toast for about 5 to 8 minutes, rotating halfway through, until they are a light golden brown. Remove the walnuts from the oven and set them aside.

3   In the work bowl of a stand mixer fitted with the paddle attachment, mix the butter on medium speed until it becomes light and airy, about 2 minutes.

4   Add the sugars and mix on medium-low speed, stopping to scrape down the work bowl as necessary, for about 5 minutes, or until the mixture becomes light and airy.

5   Meanwhile, sift the flour, salt, baking soda, and cinnamon into a separate bowl. Set the mixture aside. Peel the bananas and chop them. Set them aside.

6   Add the eggs to the butter mixture one at a time, while mixing at a low speed. Make sure the first egg is fully incorporated into the batter before adding the next one. Make sure to scrape down the side and bottom of the work bowl to ensure everything gets mixed.

7   Add the vanilla and bananas and slowly mix to incorporate. Break up the bananas, but leave a few large chunks.

8   Add the flour mixture, little by little, and mix on low speed just long enough to combine. Do not overmix, or you will have overly dense loaves. Fold in the toasted walnuts and pour the batter into the loaf pans.

9   Place the pans in the oven and bake for about 30 to 40 minutes, depending on the size of the baking vessels. When a toothpick can be inserted into the centers of the loaves and pulled out with no batter on it, the loaves are done.

10 Remove the banana bread from the oven and let the loaves cool completely before slicing.

2 cups all-purpose flour, plus more as needed

1 cup walnuts, chopped

4 oz. unsalted butter, softened and diced

⅔ cup sugar

⅔ cup brown sugar

1 teaspoon fine sea salt

1 teaspoon baking soda

1 tablespoon cinnamon

3 very ripe bananas

3 eggs

1 tablespoon pure vanilla extract

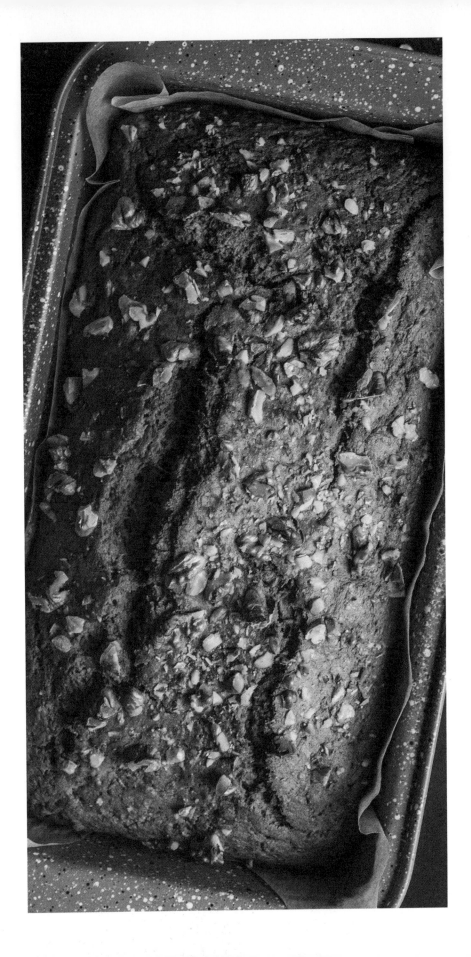

2 egg whites

¼ teaspoon kosher salt

½ teaspoon pure
vanilla extract

4 oz. sugar

2 oz. water

8 oz. unsalted butter,
softened and diced into
½-tablespoon chunks

¼ cup rainbow sprinkles,
plus more for garnish

Funfetti Cake (see page 186),
for serving

○

BIRTHDAY CAKE BUTTERCREAM WITH FUNFETTI CAKE

○

A great board for a birthday party, or any celebration.
The buttercream can be a little tricky to prepare for those who do not
bake often, but the flavor is well worth working diligently to perfect.

1   Add the egg whites, salt, and vanilla extract to the work bowl of a stand mixer fitted with the whisk attachment. Begin mixing on the lowest speed setting.

2   Add the sugar and water to a small saucepan and heat the mixture over medium-high heat, stirring to dissolve the sugar. Bring it to a steady simmer and cook the syrup until it reaches 240°F on a candy thermometer, about 7 or 8 minutes.

3   Adjust the speed of your mixer, with the egg whites in it, to medium speed, and continue to whip the egg whites until they reach soft peaks.

4   Remove the syrup from the stove, and, with the mixer running at a medium-high speed, slowly add the syrup in a thin stream to the egg whites until all of the syrup is incorporated. Try to aim the stream close to the center of the bowl, and do not add it too quickly, or you will curdle the egg whites.

5   Continue to mix the egg whites on medium-low until they become stiff and glossy and the bottom of the mixing bowl is at room temperature. Keep whipping the egg whites on low speed until the bowl has cooled back down to room temperature, 10 to 15 minutes.

6   Begin adding the butter, chunk by chunk, while the mixer is on medium speed, until all of the butter has been incorporated, waiting until each chunk is fully incorporated before adding the next one.

7   Fold in the rainbow sprinkles using a rubber spatula.

8   Spread the buttercream on a board in the desired manner, garnish with additional rainbow sprinkles, and serve with the Funfetti Cake.

FUNFETTI CAKE

5 oz. unsalted butter, softened, plus more as needed

2 cups cake flour

1 teaspoon baking powder

1 teaspoon baking soda

½ teaspoon fine sea salt

1 cup sugar

¼ cup vegetable oil

2 eggs

1 egg white

2 teaspoons pure vanilla extract

¾ cup buttermilk

½ cup rainbow sprinkles

Birthday Cake Buttercream (see page 185)

1   Preheat the oven to 350°F. Coat a round 9-inch cake pan with butter.

2   Whisk the flour, baking powder, baking soda, and salt together in a large bowl and set the mixture aside.

3   In the work bowl of a stand mixer fitted with the paddle attachment, mix the butter and sugar together on medium speed for about 5 minutes, or until the mixture has become light and airy. Use a rubber spatula to scrape down the side and bottom of the work bowl. Mix again at medium speed for another 15 to 30 seconds to ensure that all of the butter gets evenly mixed.

4   Add the oil and continue to mix for 1 minute until all of the oil is incorporated.

5   Add the eggs, egg white, and vanilla and continue to mix until everything is combined.

6   Slowly add half of the buttermilk, followed by half of the dry mixture from earlier, and mix until everything comes together. Repeat to incorporate all of the buttermilk and dry mixture, being careful not to overmix.

7   Fold in the rainbow sprinkles and pour the batter into the cake pan.

8   Place the pan in the oven and bake for 30 to 35 minutes, or until a toothpick inserted into the center of the cake comes out clean.

9   Remove the cake from the oven and let it cool in the pan for about 10 minutes. Transfer the cake to a wire rack and let it cool completely before frosting with the buttercream.

HAZELNUT SPREAD WITH BANANAS, CHOCOLATE & BEIGNETS

Even without the Beignets, this board would be epic. With them, it's entirely first-rate, and one of the most decadent boards in the entire book.

Making hazelnut butter is a lot of work and provides relatively low yield for the cost and effort. For that reason, we went ahead and used a store-bought hazelnut-chocolate spread. The most popular is certainly Nutella, but feel free to use whichever one you prefer.

4 oz. hazelnut-chocolate spread

1 ripe banana, sliced, for serving

1 oz. dark chocolate, for serving

Beignets (see page 190), for serving

1 Spread the hazelnut-chocolate spread on a board in the desired manner and serve with the banana, chocolate, and Beignets.

BEIGNETS

1   Gently heat the evaporated milk to about 90°F and stir in the 2 teaspoons of sugar until it has dissolved.

2   Whisk in the active dry yeast and set the mixture aside. The yeast should begin to foam after about 5 minutes.

3   Meanwhile, combine the flours, salt, cinnamon, and nutmeg in a bowl and set the mixture aside.

4   In the work bowl of a stand mixer fitted with the dough hook, add the mixture, the remaining sugar, and the egg and mix to combine, about 1 minute.

5   Slowly stream in the melted butter and then add the flour mixture in three increments, waiting until each addition has been incorporated before adding the next. Once you have a nice ball of dough, mix on low speed for about 4 minutes, until the dough is smooth and bounces back when you poke it.

6   Coat a bowl with butter and place the dough in it. Cover the bowl with plastic wrap and let it sit in a naturally warm place until the dough has doubled in size, about 2 hours.

7   When the dough has just about doubled in size, set up your fryer by placing the canola oil in a Dutch oven and warming it to 325°F. Set a rimmed baking sheet with a cooling rack in it beside the stove.

8   While the oil is heating, turn the dough out onto an all-purpose flour–dusted work surface. Roll it out with a rolling pin so that the sheet of dough is about ¼ inch thick. Cut the dough into roughly 16 even squares. Coat a baking sheet with butter and place the beignets on it. Allow the beignets to sit for 10 minutes.

9   Fry the beignets in batches of 4 or 5, for 2 minutes on one side, and then flip them and fry for 1 to 2 more minutes, or until the entire beignet is golden brown and no longer doughy on the inside.

10 When a beignet is finished cooking, transfer it to the cooling rack to drain the excess oil. When all of the beignets have been cooked, sprinkle confectioners' sugar over them and serve.

1 cup evaporated milk

¼ cup plus 2 teaspoons sugar

2 teaspoons active dry yeast

1¼ cups bread flour

1¼ cups all-purpose flour, plus more as needed

½ teaspoon fine sea salt

1 teaspoon cinnamon

1 teaspoon freshly grated nutmeg

1 egg

2 tablespoons unsalted butter, melted, plus more as needed

4 cups canola oil

Confectioners' sugar, for topping

PEANUT BUTTER WITH GRAPES, ROASTED PEANUTS & BREAD

An American classic, the peanut butter and jelly sandwich, is the inspiration for this board. Those fast friends are featured, and bolstered with roasted peanuts and fresh grapes to provide the board with balance.

While making peanut butter at home sounds like fun, as anyone who has made it themselves can tell you, it really isn't, and the stuff you can get in stores is comparable, if not better, than the peanut butter you will end up with. For that very reason, we have decided to go with store-bought peanut butter for this board.

While making jelly is not nearly as difficult as making peanut butter, we also went with store-bought jelly because even the best homemade versions of some recipes just can't stand up to those memories we have of childhood snacks, and nostalgia is on the menu here.

4 oz. smooth peanut butter

2 oz. grape jelly

12 to 15 grapes, sliced, for garnish

2 oz. roasted peanuts, for garnish

Bread, for serving

1 Spread the peanut butter on a board in the desired manner and top it with dollops of the grape jelly. Garnish with the grapes and peanuts and serve with bread.

LEMON & HONEY BUTTER WITH CRACKERS

Featuring fresh summer herbs and bursts of bright lemon, this board is rounded out with a touch of sweetness from some honey and a nice, complex tartness from balsamic vinegar. It's the perfect board to break out on a summer afternoon.

4 oz. unsalted butter, softened

2 teaspoons honey

Zest of 1 lemon, plus more for garnish

Juice of ½ lemon

¼ teaspoon kosher salt

Fresh mint, chopped, for garnish

Fresh basil, chopped, for garnish

Balsamic vinegar, for garnish

Crackers or bread, for serving

1 Place the butter in the work bowl of a stand mixer fitted with the paddle attachment and add the honey, lemon zest, lemon juice, and salt.

2 Mix on medium-low for about 2 minutes, or until all of the ingredients have evenly blended into the butter.

3 Use a rubber spatula to scrape down the side and bottom of the work bowl. Mix again at medium speed for another 15 to 30 seconds to ensure that all of the butter gets evenly incorporated.

4 Spread the butter on a board in the desired manner. Garnish with additional lemon zest, mint, basil, and balsamic vinegar, and serve with crackers or bread.

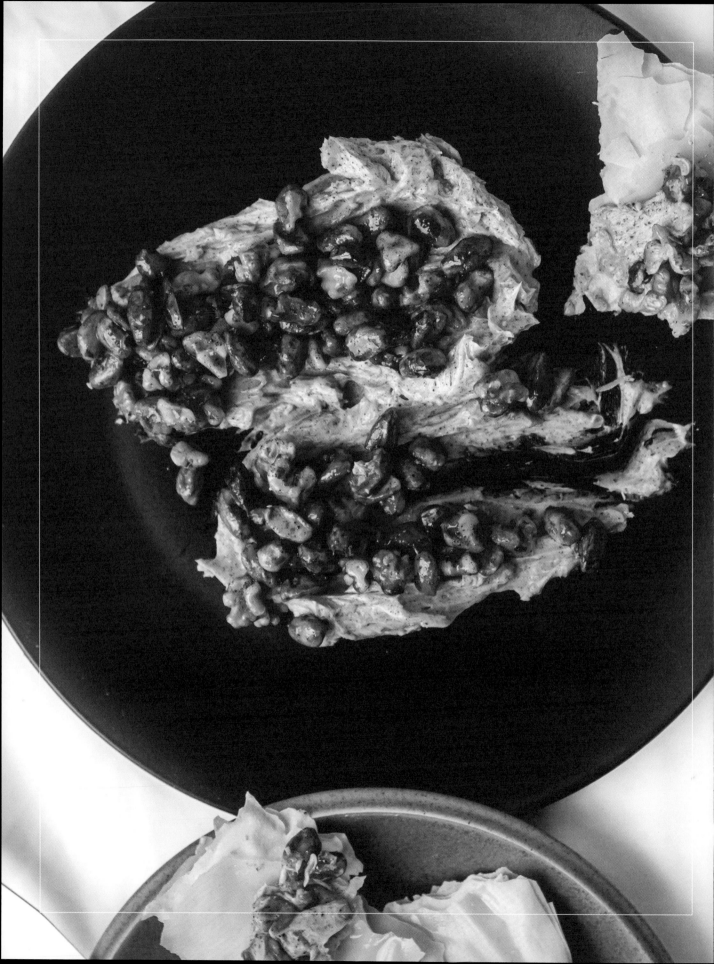

BAKLAVA BUTTER WITH KATAIFI

This board is essentially a deconstructed baklava, a traditional Greek dessert consisting of sweetened and spiced nuts layered between sheets of buttery phyllo dough. Because of that dish's inherent richness, it's a natural to turn into a butter board.

4 oz. unsalted butter, softened

1 teaspoon cinnamon

1 teaspoon honey

¼ teaspoon ground cloves

¼ teaspoon kosher salt

Baklava Topping (see page 198), for garnish

Phyllo dough, baked, for serving

1 Place the butter in the work bowl of a stand mixer fitted with the paddle attachment and add the cinnamon, honey, cloves, and salt.

2 Mix on medium-low for about 1 minute, or until all of the ingredients have evenly blended into the butter.

3 Use a rubber spatula to scrape down the side and bottom of the work bowl. Mix again at medium speed for another 15 to 30 seconds to ensure that all of the butter gets evenly incorporated.

4 Spread the butter on a board in the desired manner. Garnish with the Baklava Topping and serve with phyllo dough.

BAKLAVA TOPPING

2 oz. walnuts, toasted

2 oz. pistachios, toasted

1 oz. honey

1 teaspoon cinnamon

¼ teaspoon ground cloves

Zest of 1 lemon

2 pinches of kosher salt

1 Add the toasted walnuts and pistachios to a small bowl and drizzle with the honey, followed by the cinnamon and cloves.

2 Toss to coat, and then add the lemon zest and salt. Toss again to evenly distribute the ingredients among the nuts and serve.

METRIC CONVERSIONS

US Measurement	Approximate Metric Liquid Measurement	Approximate Metric Dry Measurement
1 teaspoon	5 ml	5 g
1 tablespoon or ½ ounce	15 ml	14 g
1 ounce or ⅛ cup	30 ml	29 g
¼ cup or 2 ounces	60 ml	57 g
⅓ cup	80 ml	76 g
½ cup or 4 ounces	120 ml	113 g
⅔ cup	160 ml	151 g
¾ cup or 6 ounces	180 ml	170 g
1 cup or 8 ounces or ½ pint	240 ml	227 g
1½ cups or 12 ounces	350 ml	340 g
2 cups or 1 pint or 16 ounces	475 ml	454 g
3 cups or 1½ pints	700 ml	680 g
4 cups or 2 pints or 1 quart	950 ml	908 g

INDEX

ABOUT the AUTHORS

Alejandra and Jamison are a wife-and-husband duo with a love for bringing restaurant-caliber recipes into the home kitchen. Having first met while working at a farm-to-table restaurant, they have a deep passion for the culinary industry that translates to their everyday lives.

Alejandra is a food photographer and stylist, and Jamie is a trained chef and recipe developer with 15+ years of experience at restaurants such as The Inn at Little Washington and Market Table Bistro. Their blog, Off the Line, is packed with recipes that are fresh, feature seasonal ingredients, and integrate classic cooking techniques. The blog is focused on being approachable for the home cook, like Alejandra, and remarkable for the chef inside all of us, like Jamie.

Based in Northern Virginia, they enjoy visiting the best wineries and breweries around, taking daily walks, and exploring locally sourced ingredients. They believe that each meal, no matter how simple or elaborate, deserves to be a special moment that inspires.

ABOUT CIDER MILL PRESS
BOOK PUBLISHERS

Good ideas ripen with time. From seed to harvest, Cider Mill Press brings fine reading, information, and entertainment together between the covers of its creatively crafted books. Our Cider Mill bears fruit twice a year, publishing a new crop of titles each spring and fall.

"Where Good Books Are Ready for Press"
501 Nelson Place
Nashville, Tennessee 37214

cidermillpress.com